IGNORANCE IS NO EXCUSE

by Estell Evelyn Williams

Dorrance Publishing Co., Inc.
701 Smithfield Street
Pittsburgh, PA 15222
Visit our website at *www.dorrancebookstore.com*

ISBN: 978-1-4809-0551-1
eISBN: 978-1-4809-0545-0

The material contained herein was written and edited by Estell E. Williams, a Worldwide Street Minister, as she was inspired and directed by God - Titles and Contents.

Registration Number: TXu 1-677-868

The picture on the cover of this book is an actual and true picture of our Lord and Saviour, Jesus Christ, taken through an airplane window by an Evangelist's associate as soon as He appeared in the sky after the Evangelist asked Him to let her see Him.

All scripture contained herein are from the 1611 Authorized Version of the King James Bible. Add thou not unto His words, lest He reprove thee and thou be found a liar (Prov. 30:6).

Any and everything you could ever want to know, and the answer to any and every question you could have ever have, is in that version. If you read any other book (version), you are reading another man's opinion. "What I have spoken, I have spoken, Nothing is to be added to it nor taken from it," saith God.

"If it's new, it's not true."

"I know the end from the beginning," saith God to the writer. Also, "I love those who were born for life unto life and those who were born for death unto death."

PREFACE

This book, "IGNORANCE IS NO EXCUSE," contains five (5) books with different information spiritually gathered by the author over a period of two (2) years beginning 1992 to 1994 at the direct guidance from God. They provide historical facts; the truth about the creation of man; gives you the words from God to live by; and, will assist you with your spiritual growth.

God has informed the author that the current immoral conditions in the entire world today are due solely to the lack of spiritual knowledge and the keeping of his statues, judgments and Commandments. Also, that because of this, the current days are the same as in the days of Noah. "I am weary of repenting," saith God; and, that "America has left Him. If they would return, He would heal their land." The author has been lead to put most of His words in this book through the use of scriptures taken from the 1611 authorized King James Version of the Bible. *"If you read any other version, you are reading another man's opinion. What I have spoken, I have spoken. Nothing is to be added to it nor taken from it,"* saith God.

The author believes that we must also know the reality of the indwelling Spirit. This book is for those who have not read nor studied the Word of God. It is also for those who do not know that we are not only living under grace, but under the entire Word of God, from Genesis to Revelation.

The author has juxtaposed her strong love for the Word of God with the study of the origin of man, as she was guided by God. God continually tells her *"The truth will be made known;" "My people are perishing for lack of knowledge;" "Go to the Jew first, then to the Gentile."* As she was trying to find a way to get to Israel, He said "Africa." She was then led to purchase a video—*"Lost Tribes of Israel (Jacob)."* This video told her the truth about the origin of the Jew and enlightened her further on the beginning of man and the country where we are all descended from. Other reference materials were also selected by God to provide her with factual information on this subject, which is presented in this book.

One compelling day, He asked the author to turn on her television. She obeyed and saw dead Africans from AIDS all over what appeared to have been the entire continent of Africa. He immediately reminded her that *"Their blood will be on your hands,"* words spoken by Him to her when she delayed her trip to Africa. She was also reminded at that time of His words *"Many of My chosen are not going to make it."* In 1998, she finally got a chance to go with a ministerial group up the coast of East Africa by ship from Dublin to Tanzania. Afterwards, she made several more ministerial trips: to Israel in 2005 and 2007 and to Ghana and Acura in 2008. These trips continued to enlighten her about the origin of man and the plight of mankind due to his disobedience to the Word of God.

It has been proven that the AIDS virus was man-made to annihilate all Negroes from the face of the earth. *"A remnant will be saved to replenish the land,"* saith God to the author. This statement was repeated again to her in January 2000.

The history of the African continent (the record of man) can be traced to a past more distant than of any other continent. Africa is most certainly the birthplace of mankind. If certain Biblical passages, especially in the Old Testament, seem absurd, this is because recording specialists were unable to accept the evidentiary proof for their own personal reasons. The author believes that this is why God has guided her to present her books "From The Beginning" and "The Negro" with this truth first. His scriptures in the books "The Forgotten Thou Shalt Nots" and "Little Foxes," are to anchor you spiritually; and, "Just Quotes" are from Him to the author over a period of several years, to help you live your daily life in the Spirit.

This book is dedicated to all mankind.

The "Lost Tribes of Israel" video:
WGBH Boston Video
P.O. Box 2284
South Burlington, VT 05407–2284

Telephone: 1-(800) 949-8670; Fax (802) 864-9846
www.wgbh.org
Computer & Technology - CNET.com

The Bible contains the mind of God, the state of men, the way of salvation, the doom of sinners, and the happiness of believers. Its doctrine is holy, its precepts are binding, its histories are true, and its decisions are immutable. Read it to be wise, believe it to be safe, and practice it to be holy.

It contains light to direct you, food to support you, and comfort to cheer you. It is the traveler's map, the pilgrim's staff, the pilot's compass, the soldier's sword, and the Christian's charter.

Here Paradise is restored, heaven opened, and ways of hell disclosed. Christ is its grand object, our good its design, and the redemption of man its end. It should fill the memory, rule the heart, and guide the feet. It is a mine of wealth, a paradise of glory, a river of pleasure.

It is given to you in life, will be open in the judgment, and will be remembered forever. It involves the highest responsibilities, will reward the greatest labor, and condemn all who trifle with its sacred contents.

Author Unknown

CONTENTS

BOOK I

If you have any disagreement with the contents of Book I and Book II, let them be known to God and not this writer. For it was He who chose the books from which the information was taken out of that He wanted them to contain. Also, it was He who gave me the titles He wanted them to have.

References:
"Africa to 1875-A Modern History"
Robin Hallett @ Ann Arbor: The University of Michigan Press 1970

"The African Origin of Civilization, Myth or Reality"
Diop Cheikhanta © Lawrence Hill & Co, 1974

FROM THE BEGINNING

THE NEGRO
ADAM
The Beginning of Mankind
The First Son of God

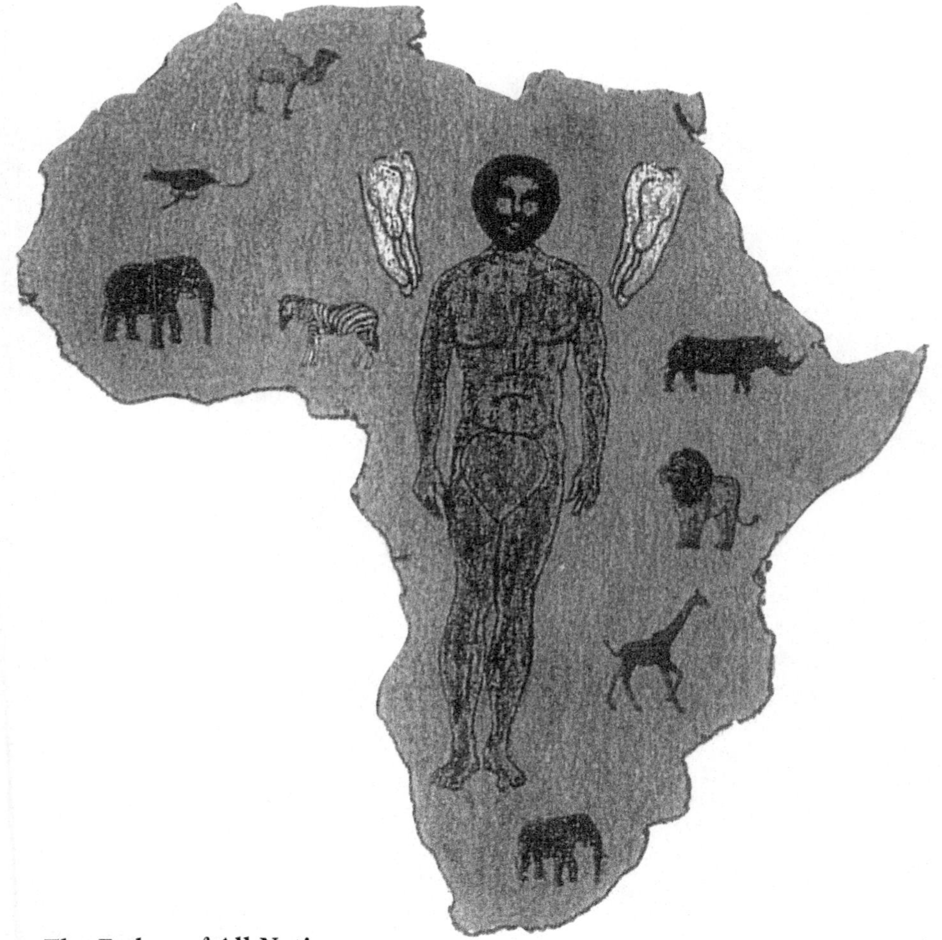

The Father of All Nations

Genesis 2:7 And the Lord God formed man of the dust of the ground, and breathed into his nostrils the breath of life; and man became a living soul.

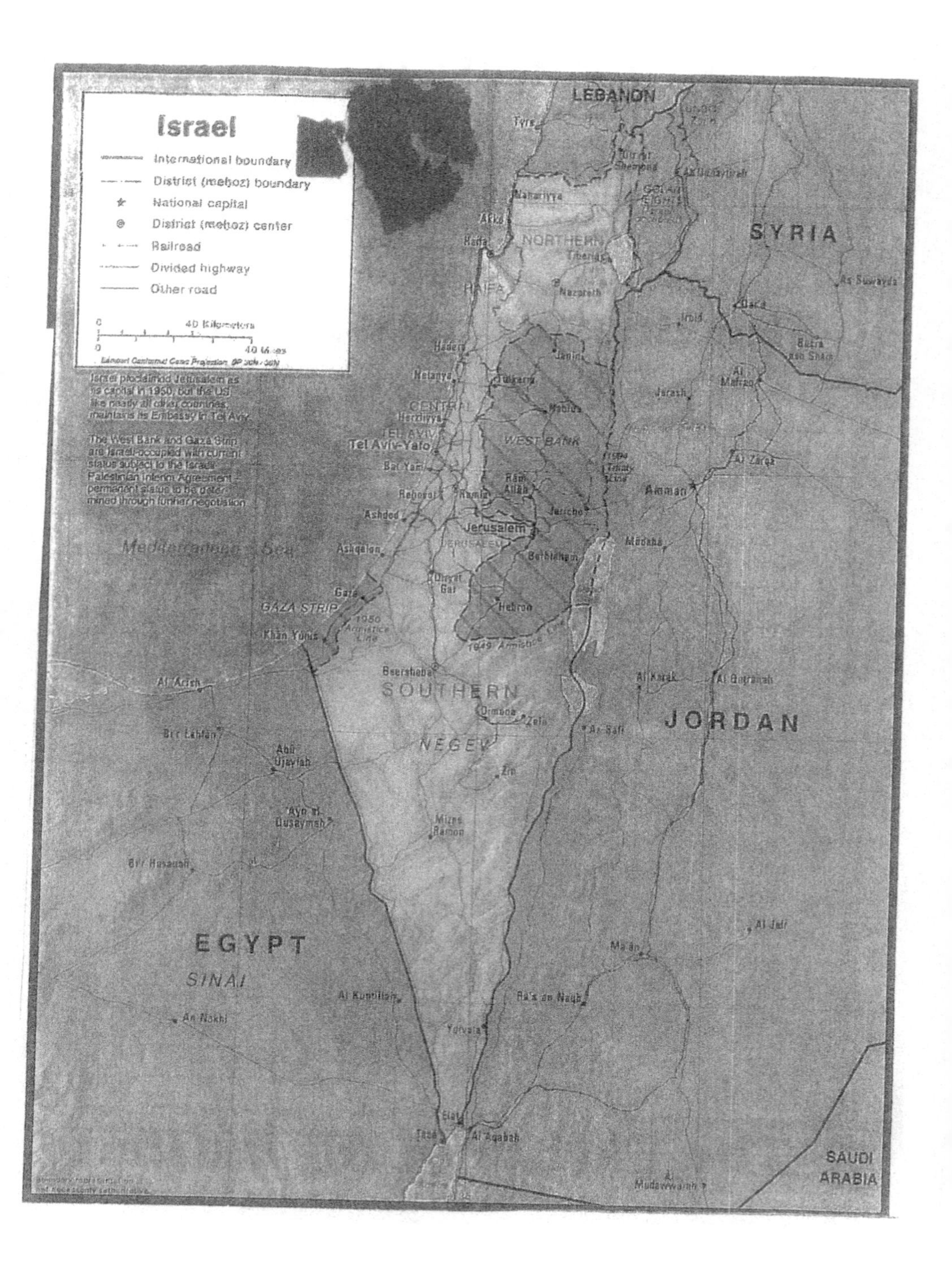
Israel
International boundary
District (mehoz) boundary
National capital
District (mehoz) center
Railroad
Divided highway
Other road
0
40 Kilometers
0
Israel proclaimed Jerusalem as its capital in 1950, but the US, like nearly all other countries, maintains its Embassy in Tel Aviv.
The West Bank and Gaza Strip are Israeli-occupied with current status subject to the Israeli-Palestinian Interim Agreement - permanent status to be determined through further negotiation.
LEBANON
Tyre
Nahariyya
Akko
Haifa
NORTHERN
Tiberias
HAIFA
Nazareth
SYRIA
As Suwayda
Dar'a
Irbid
Hadera
Jenin
Netanya
Tulkarm
Al Mafraq
Jarash
CENTRAL
Herzliyya
Nablus
TEL AVIV
Tel Aviv-Yafo
WEST BANK
Bat Yam
Az Zarqa
Rehovot
Ramla
Amman
Ashdod
Jericho
Jerusalem
Mediterranean Sea
Ashqelon
Bethlehem
Madaba
Gaza
GAZA STRIP
Hebron
Khan Yunis
1949 Armistice Line
Beersheba
SOUTHERN
Al Karak
Al Qatranah
Al 'Arish
Dimona
Zefa
JORDAN
NEGEV
Zin
Mizpe Ramon
EGYPT
SINAI
Al Kuntillah
Ra's an Naqb
An Nakhl
Yotvata
Al Jafr
Eilat
Al 'Aqabah
SAUDI
ARABIA

The Lord came from Sinai (Egypt) and rose up from Seir unto them (Deut 33:2). Before me there was no God formed neither shall there be after me (Isa 54:10). I am the Lord thy God from the land of Egypt, thou shalt know no God but me; for there is no saviour besides me (Hosea 13:4). Their bodies shall lie in the street of the great city which is spiritually called Sodom of Egypt, WHERE ALSO OUR LORD WAS CRUCIFIED (Rev 11:8).

8. Mycerinus (Fourth Dynasty), who built the third Giza pyramid. Next to him, the goddess Hathor.

FROM THE BEGINNING

HISTORY OF ETHIOPIA

"Humanlike fossils have been found in the Danakil depression dating back 3.5 million years; in 1981, the 4-million-year-old fossil bones of a direct ancestor of Homo sapiens were discovered in the Awash River Valley. Evidence of cereal agriculture dates back to about 5000 B.C. Homer refers to the Ethiopians as a "blameless race" and Herodotus claims that they were known in his time as the "most just men."

AFRICA to 1875, Chapter III

"To grasp the history of the African continent is a formidable undertaking. Not only is Africa very large and very varied, but the record of man can be traced to a past more distant than that in any other continent. In the Americas human history begins a mere thirty thousand years ago; in Africa the remains of the earliest known tool-making hominids are now reckoned to be close to two million years old.

Africa appears almost certainly to have been the birthplace of mankind. This hypothesis was first put forward a century ago by Charles Darwin, who based his argument on what was then known as the distribution of higher apes. The fossil remains of early hominids discovered in East and South Africa go far to confirm Darwin's hypothesis. The fossil remains found in Kenya in 1963, of a creature known provisionally as Kenyapithecus wicker and regarded as being a member of the family Hominidae, date back at least twelve million years.

Of all the African sites that have produced evidence of early hominids, Olduval Gorge is at once the most spectacular and the most informative. Olduval lies in one of the wildest and most arid parts of East Africa...The gorge, a great gash in the floor of the Rift Valley...cutting down through three thousand feet of ancient lake sediments and thus exposing, neatly stratified, layer upon layer of deposits rich with the remains of the lake-side camps of generations of early man.

THE AFRICAN ORIGIN OF CIVILIZATION

Meaning of Our Work-p. xv

2. Anthropologically and culturally speaking, the Semitic world was born during protohistoric times from the mixture of white-skinned and black-skinned people in western Asia. This is why an understanding of the Mesopotamian Semitic world, Judaic or Arabic, requires constant reference to the underlying Black reality. If certain Biblical passages, especially in the Old Testament, seem absurd, this is because specialists,

puffed up with prejudices, are unable to accept documentary evidence.

3. The triumph of the monogenetic thesis of humanity (Leaky), even at the stage of "Homo Sapiens-Sapiens," compels one to admit that all races descended from the Black race, according to a filiation process that science will one day explain.

CHAPTER I - What Were the Egyptians?

In contemporary descriptions of the ancient Egyptians, this question is never raised. Eyewitnesses of that period formally affirm that the Egyptians were Black.

The opinion of all the ancient writers on the Egyptian race is more or less summed up by Gaston Maspero (1846–1916): "By the almost unanimous testimony of ancient historians, they belonged to an African race (read: Negro which first settled in Ethiopia, on the middle of the Nile).

According to the Bible, Egypt was peopled by the offspring of Ham, ancestor of the Blacks. What is the value of these statements? Coming from eyewitnesses, they could hardly be false.

CHAPTER XIII - Early History of Humanity: Evolution of the Black World

The Negro has been there since the beginning of time, p. 274

The Negro has been there from the beginning; for the millennia he was the only one in existence. P. 274

HOMO - (Gk - same)

SAPIENT- (Lat - Sapiens) Wise; full of knowledge; sagacious; often ironical.

From this writer

All of the preceding indicates that the Garden of Eden was/is located in Africa.

Why did all of the events and the people who are written about in the beginning of the Bible occur in the dark continent of Africa and move or journey toward Arabia, which was most likely a part of the country of Africa during that time and has remained a country of Black people, if the origin of civilization did not begin in Africa?

14. Egyptian Woman.

Would anyone who does not believe in/on the Lord Jesus Christ as their Lord and Saviour today be a chosen people of God? Maybe. Or, that He is yet to come? Again, maybe.

ACTS 17:24. God that made the world and all things therein, seeing that he is Lord of heaven and earth

26. And hath made of ONE BLOOD all nations of men for to dwell on all the face of the earth, and hath determined the times before appointed, and the bounds of their habitation;

Since God made all men from one blood (Acts 17:26), and the origin of man has been established by extensive work of archeologists and anthropologists to have been Africa, does not all men/races have the blood of Africans flowing through their veins? "One drop...? As it has been determined by...? Then even the blood of Jesus that washes us from all of our sins is of that same blood, is it not?

Does not God consider all of us to be brothers and sisters? Is not three-fourths of the population of the world of color? Straight-haired or wooly?

"A great people have nothing to do with petty history." P. xvi

Let us accept the things that we cannot change, and change the things that we can. For instance, our relationship with OUR Father, which will automatically change our relationship with each other.

GENESIS 1:26. And God said, "Let us make man in our image, after our likeness:"

27. So god created man in his own image...male and female created he them.

28. And God blessed them, and God said unto them, be fruitful, and multiply, and replenish the earth, and subdue it.

31. And God saw every thing that he had made, and, behold, it was very good.

GENESIS 2:8. And the Lord God planted a garden eastward in Eden,

10. And a river went out of Eden to water the garden; and from thence it was parted, and became into four heads, (the four races, maybe? Black, Red, Yellow, White?)

11. The name of the first is Pison: that is it which compasseth the whole land of Havilah, where there is gold (Africa);

13. And the name of the second river is Gihon: the same is it that compasseth the whole land of Ethiopia (Africa).

14. And the name of the third river is Hiddekel: that is it which goeth toward the east of Assyria (the current country of Arabia), and the fourth river is Euphrates (also the current country of Arabia).

15. And the Lord God took the man (Adam) and put him into the Garden of Eden to dress it and to keep it.

Is not Egypt the most dominant country mentioned in the Bible where most all of the people who God used to accomplish his plan for the world and for mankind, from Adam to...? located in Africa?

MATTHEW 2:13. And when they were departed, behold, the angel of the Lord appeareth to Joseph in a dream, saying, "Arise, and take the young child (JESUS) and his mother, and flee into Egypt... (AFRICA)."

Was Bethlehem of Judea, the birthplace of Jesus, located in a country of Africa during that time? I have not been able to locate this information. The current country of India is steadily drifting away from her mother country, Africa. Could not the present countries of Israel and Arabia also have done the same thing in another form of separation? Their lands are still connected to Africa. Much information containing the truth of this matter is buried somewhere in our libraries and not made available to the peoples of the world.

Does not the current country of Israel—which was Canaan the land of the descendants of Ham, the reputed ancestor of the SEMITIC Blacks—lie between Africa and Arabia?

I raise these questions because ten years ago when God gave the following commandments to me— "Bring my people out of bondage;" "Teach the children because adult minds are set and cannot be changed;" "Go to the lost sheep of Israel (Jacob?) first, then to the Gentiles;" —the only country He spoke to me was, "Africa."

As I was trying to think of a Jewish Synagogue that would permit me to minister there, He said, "My people are perishing for lack of knowledge." Later, "Many of my chosen are not going to make it."

He reminded me of these last words during the Desert Storm war when the scud missile destroyed the building(s) where the recent arrival of American soldiers were. The 'children'— now young men— that I was supposed to have taught, or to have been instrumental in leading to the Lord.

Because of previous teachings, and His use of the words "chosen" and "lost sheep of Israel," I thought that He was referring to the country of Israel. That is, until He inspired me to put this book together, provided me with the material that He wanted it to contain, and gave me its title.

In view of all of the preceding, who are the REAL CHOSEN PEOPLE OF GOD? And, who are the REAL HEBREWS OR JEWS? The 'blameless race' and "most just men," or...? Is not God blameless and just?

GENESIS 3:20. And Adam called his wife's name Eve; because SHE WAS THE MOTHER OF ALL LIVING (all mankind).

22. And the Lord God said, .Behold, the man is become as one of us, to know good and evil.

23. Therefore, the Lord God sent him forth from the Garden of Eden, to till the ground from whence he was taken.

GENESIS 5:28. Lamech (son of Methusael; a descendant of Cain, Adams' firstborn) begat a son:

29. And he called his name Noah, saying, this same shall comfort us concerning our work and toil of our hands, because of the ground which the Lord hath cursed.

32. ...Noah begat Shem, ham, and Japheth

GENESIS 9:1. And God blessed Noah and his sons... (Africans)

19. ....and of them was the whole earth overspread.

From the Writer

Is not the condition of the world today as it was in the days of Noah? God has said it is.

March 1992, 3:30 a.m. - REPENT ALL YE LAND!! PREPARE THE WAY FOR THE LORD!! TAKE HEED!!

BOOK II

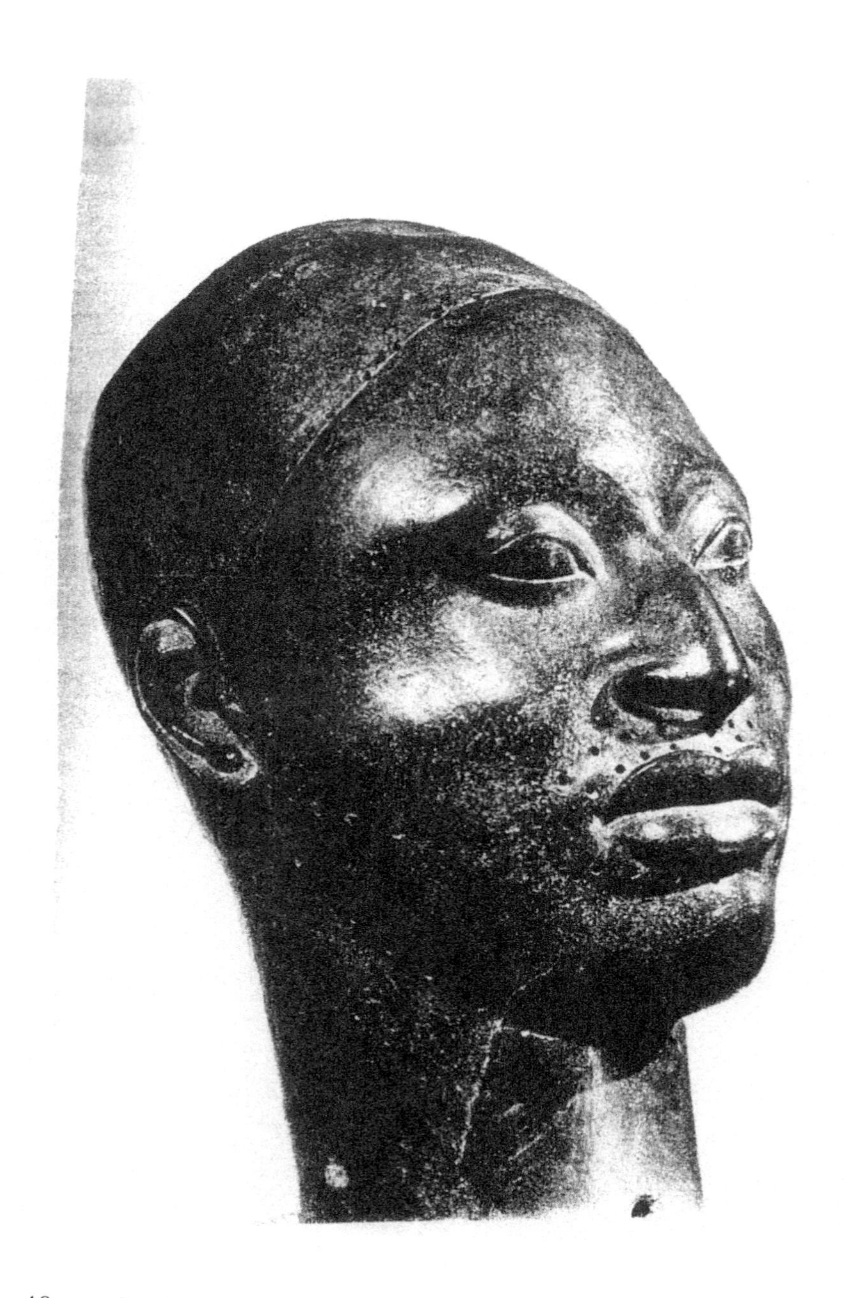

40. Benin Bronze Head: "Court Dignitary" (British Museum cast, Nigeria). (Courtesy of the American Museum of Natural History.)

THE NEGRO

The contents of this book will only be accepted by an open and "superior" mind.

"I made all things in six days," saith God to this writer. Black man, White woman; both native Africans. Adam from the black soil of Africa, Eve from the white rib bone of Adam. (Genesis 2:7, 21–24)

Since from the beginning God made only one man and one woman, and from the beginning made of "one blood" all nations of men for to dwell on all the face of the earth (Acts 17:26), then every human being that has ever existed or even now exist, descended from that Black man and White woman and have that "one blood" flowing through their veins, do they not? Would not this then make every nation of Negro origin? And every one a Negro?

AFRICA TO 1875

CHAPTER III - Periods of African History

FROM 1,750,000 TO 50,000 YEARS AGO

Africa appears almost certainly to have been the birthplace of mankind. This hypothesis was first put forward a century ago by Charles Darwin. The fossil remains of early hominids discovered in East and South Africa go far to confirm Darwin's hypothesis.

ETHIOPIA - "History"

Homer - (Greek poet) - refers to the Ethiopians as a "blameless race," and Herodotus - (Greek historian) - claims that they were known in his time as the "most just men." (484? - 425? B.C.)

THE AFRICAN ORIGIN OF CIVILIZATION

Myth or Realty, Meaning of Our Work p xv

3. The triumph of the monogenetic thesis of humanity (Leaky), even at the stage of "Homo Sapiens-Sapiens," compels one to admit that all races descended from the Black race, according to a filiation process that science will one day explain.

6. A great people have nothing to do with petty history. (p.xvi)

CHAPTER I - What Were the Egyptians?

The opinion of all ancient writers on the Egyptian race is more or less summed up by Gaston Maspero (1846–1916): "By the almost unanimous testimony of ancient historians, they belonged to an African race (read: Negro) which first settled in Ethiopia, on the middle Nile (p.2).

According to the Bible, Egypt was peopled by the offspring of Ham, ancestor of the Blacks (p2).

CHAPTER II - **Birth of the Negro Myth**

Ruined by successive invasions, Egypt, the cradle of civilization for 10,000 years would no longer play a political role. Nevertheless, it would long continue to initiate the younger Mediterranean peoples (Greek and Romans, among others) into the enlightenment of civilization. Throughout antiquity it would remain the classic land where the Mediterranean peoples went on pilgrimages to drink at the fount of scientific, religious, moral, and social knowledge, the most ancient such knowledge that mankind had acquired. (p.10).

When Egypt lost its independence, their isolation was complete. (p.23)

From then on, separated from the mother country which was invaded by the foreigner, and withdrawn in a geographical setting requiring a minimum effort of adjustment, the Blacks were oriented toward the development of their social, political, and moral organization, rather than toward speculative scientific research that their circumstances failed to justify, and even rendered impossible. Adaptation to the narrow, fertile Nile Valley required expert technique in irrigation and dams, precise calculations to foresee the inundations of the Nile and to deduce their economics and social consequences. It also required the invention of geometry to delimit property after the floods obliterated boundary lines. By the same token the terrain in long flat strips required the transformation of the paleo-Negritic hoe into a plow, first drawn by man, subsequently by animals. Since history had disrupted his former equilibrium with the environment, the Black now found a new equilibrium, differing from the first in the absence of a technique no longer vital to the social, political, and moral organization. With economic resources assured by means that did not require perpetual inventions, the Negro became progressively indifferent to material progress.

It was under these new conditions that the encounter with Europe took place. In the fifteenth century, when the first Portuguese, Dutch, English, French, Danes, and Brandenburgers began to set up trading posts on the West African Coast, the political organization of the African States was equal, and often superior, to that of their own respective States. (p.23)

African was therefore quite vulnerable from the technical standpoint. It became tempting, irresistible prey for the West, provided with firearms and far-ranging navies. So the economic progress of Renaissance Europe spurred on the conquest of Africa, which was rapidly accomplished, it passed from the stage of coastal trading to that of annexation by Western international agreements, followed by armed conquest called "pacification." (p.24)

12. Pharaoh Tuthmosis III, son of a Sudanese woman, founded the Eighteenth Dynasty and inaugurated the era of Egyptian imperialism. He is sometimes referred to as the "Napoleon of Antiquity."

At the beginning of this period America was discovered by Christopher Columbus and the overflow of the old continent was dumped on the new. The development of Virgin Islands required cheap labor. Defenseless Africa then became the readymade reservoir from which to draw that labor force with minimum expense and risk. The modern Negro slave trade was considered an economic necessity prior to the advent of the machine. This would last until the mid-nineteenth century. (p.24)

Such a reversal of roles, the result of new technical relations, brought with it master-slave relationships between Whites and Blacks on the social level. (p.24)

Inflated by their recent technical superiority, the Europeans looked down on the Black world and condescended to touch nothing but its' riches. Ignorance of the Black's ancient history, differences of mores and customs, ethnic prejudices between two races that believed themselves to be facing each other for the first time, combined with the economic necessity to exploit - so many factors predisposed the mind of the European to distort the moral personality of the Black and his intellectual aptitudes. (p.24)

Henceforth, "Negro" became a synonym for primitive being, inferior, endowed with a pre-logical mentality. As the human being is always eager to justify his conduct, they went even further. The desire to legitimize colonization and the slave trade - in other words, the social condition of the Negro in the modern world - engendered an entire literature to describe the so-called inferior traits of the Black. The mind of several generations of Europeans would thus be gradually indoctrinated, Western opinion would crystallize and instinctively accept as revealed truth the equation: Negro = inferior humanity. To crown this cynicism, colonization would be depicted as a duty of humanity. They invoked "the civilizing mission" of the West charged with the responsibility to raise the African to the level of other men (known to us as "the white man's burden"). From then on, capitalism had clear sailing to practice the most ferocious exploitation under the cloak of moral pretexts. (pp 24 & 25)

This climate of alienation finally deeply affected the personality of the Negro, especially the educated Black who had had an opportunity to become conscious of world opinion about him and his people. It often happens that the Negro intellectual loses confidence in his own possibilities and in those of his race to such an extent that, despite the validity of the evidence presented in this book, it will not be astonishing if some of us are still unable to believe that Blacks really played the earliest civilizing role in the world. (p.25)

The memory of the recent slavery to which the Black race has been subjected, cleverly kept alive in men's minds and especially to Black minds, often affects Black consciousness negatively. From that recent slavery, an attempt has been made to construct—despite all historical truth—a legend that the Black has always been reduced to slavery by the superior White race with which he has lived, wherever it may have been. This enables whites easily to justify the presence of Negroes in Egypt or in Mesopotamia or Arabia, by decreeing that they were enslaved. Although such an affirmation is nothing but dogma designed to falsify history— those who advance it are fully aware that it is erroneous—it nonetheless contributes to alienating Black consciousness. (p.26)

Throughout these transformations in the Negro's relations with the rest of the world it became increasingly difficult each day and even inadmissible, for those unaware of his past glory—and for Blacks themselves—to believe that they could have originated the first civilization which flowered on earth, a civilization to which humanity owes most of its progress. (pp. 26 & 27)

Just think that this race of black men, today our slave and the object of our scorn, is the very race to which we owe our arts, sciences, and even the use of speech! Just imagine finally, that it is in the midst of peoples who call themselves the greatest friends of liberty and humanity that one has approved the most barbarous slavery and questioned whether black men have the same kind of intelligence as Whites! (p. 28)

CHAPTER VIII - Arguments against a Negro Origin

In the Nile Valley, civilization resulted from man's adaptation to that particular milieu. As declared by the Ancients and by the Egyptians themselves, it originated in Nubian. This is confirmed by our knowledge that the basic elements of Egyptian civilization are neither in lower Egypt, nor in Asia, nor in Europe, but in Nubian and the heart of Africa. (p. 158)

The Egyptians usually measured the height of the flood waters with a "Nilometer," and from it they deduced the annual yield of the harvests by mathematical calculation. The calendar and astronomy also resulted from that sedentary farm life. Adaptation to the physical surrounding gave birth to certain hygienic measures: mummification (to avoid epidemics of the plague from the Delta), fasting, diets, and so on, which gradually led to medicine coming into existence. The development of social life and exchanges required the invention and use of writing. (pp. 158 & 159)

An authentic hieroglyphic writing called Njoya exists in the Cameroon...it is exactly the same type of writing as Egyptian hieroglyphics....in Sierra Leone, there is a type of writing— Vai, which is syllabic. The writing of the Bassa is cursive. That of the Nsibidi is alphabetical. (Cf. Baumann & Westermann, op, it., p. 444.) (p. 160)

Thus, it can be said that until the fifteenth century, Black Africa never lost its civilization. (p. 160)

Frobenius reports: The idea of the "barbaric Negro" is a European invention that boomeranged and dominated Europe until the start of the century. (p. 160)

<u>CHAPTER XI</u> - Contribution of Ethiopia-Nubian and Egypt

According to the unanimous testimony of the Ancients, first the Ethiopians and then the Egyptians created and raised to an extraordinary stage of development all the elements of civilization. (p. 230)

It is impossible to stress all that the world owed to the Egyptians. The Greeks merely continued and developed, sometimes partially, what the Egyptians had invented. (p.230)

Amelineau, Abbe Emile, French archeologist and professor of the History of Religions: "I fail to see why ancient Greece should reap all the honor for ideas she borrowed from Egypt." (p.232)

Egypt was indeed the classic land where two-thirds of the Greek scholars went to study. In reality, it can be said that, during the Hellenistic epoch, Alexandria was the intellectual center of the world. (p.232)

Even Greek architecture has its roots in Egypt. (p.232)

Since the Egyptian origin of civilization and the extensive borrowing of the Greeks from the Egyptians are historically evident, we may well wonder with Amelineau why, despite those facts, most people stress the role played by Greece while overlooking that of Egypt. The reason for this attitude can be detected merely by recalling the root of the question. As Egypt is a Negro country, with a civilization created by Blacks, any thesis tending to prove the contrary would have no future. (p.234)

When we say that the ancestors of the Blacks, who today live mainly in Black Africa, were the first to invent mathematics, astronomy, the calendar, sciences in general, arts, religion, agriculture, social organization, medicine, writing, technique, architecture; that they were the first to erect buildings out of 6 million tons of stone (the Great Pyramid) as architects and engineers—not simply as unskilled laborers; that they built the immense temple of Karnack, that forest of columns with its famed hypostyle hall large enough to hold Notre-Dame and its towers; that they sculpted the first colossal statutes (Colossi of Mammon, etc.) when we say all that we are merely expressing the plain unvarnished truth that no one can refute by arguments worthy of the name. (p.234)

Consequently, the Black man must become able to restore the continuity of his national historic past, to draw from it the moral advantage needed to re-conquer his place in the modern world. (p.235)

From this writer

In view of <u>all</u> of the preceding: The "Minority?" Who are they? Was not Adam made in the image and likeness of God? Then what makes one nation of people think that they have the right to say to another nation of people you are inferior to us because your skin is darker than ours? Black is Black! That one blood (God's Blood) establishes that truth. Considering the illogical reason for the application of the synonym, "Negro," it is far past the time for all of the history of man to be revised and the truth be made known. Are not three-fourths of the people in the world of Color? Straight-haired or wooly?

BOOK III

This book is for those who have not read or studied the Word of God; or, for those who have, and have for one reason or another forgotten the THOU SHALT NOTS.

It is also for those who do not know that we are not only living under grace, but under the entire Word of God, from Genesis to Revelation. FOR THE LORD HATH SPOKEN IT.

THE FORGOTTEN THOU SHALT NOTS

LEVITICUS 19:17. THOU SHALT NOT hate thy brother in thine heart: thou shalt in any wise rebuke thy neighbor, and not suffer sin upon him.

MATTHEW 7:12. Therefore all things whatsoever ye would that men should do to you, do you even so to them: for this is the law and the prophets.

ROMANS 13:8. Owe no man anything, but to love one another: for he that loveth another hath fulfilled the law.

GALATIANS 5:13. For, brethren, ye have been called unto liberty: only use not liberty for an occasion to the flesh, but by love serve one another.

14. For all the law is fulfilled in one word, even in this: Thou shalt love thy neighbor as thyself.

15. But if ye bite and devour one another, take heed that ye be not consumed one of another.

16. This I say then, Walk in the Spirit, and ye shall not fulfill the lust of the flesh.

LEVITICUS 19:18. THOU SHALT NOT avenge nor bear any grudge against the children of thy people: but thou shalt love thy neighbor as thyself: I am The Lord.

LUKE 6:27. But I say unto you which hear, Love your enemies, and do good to them which hate you.

28. Bless them that curse you, and pray for them which despitefully use you.

29. And unto him that smiteth thee on the one cheek offer also the other: and him that taketh away thy cloak forbid not to take thy coat also.

30. Give to every one that asketh of thee; and of him that taketh away thy goods ask them not again.

31. And as ye would that men should do to you, do ye also to them likewise.

32. For if ye love them which love you, what thank have ye? For even sinners also love those that love them.

33. And if ye do good to them which do good to you, what thank have

ye? For sinners also do even the same.

34. And if ye lend to them of whom ye hope to receive, what thank have ye? For sinners also lend to sinners, to receive again as much.

35. But love your enemies, and do good, and lend hoping for nothing again; and your reward shall be great and ye shall be the children of the Highest for he is kind unto the unthankful and to the evil.

36. Be ye therefore merciful as your Father also is merciful.

37. Judge not, and ye shall not be judged: condemn not, and ye shall not be condemned: forgive and ye shall be forgiven.

ROMANS 12:17. Recompense to no man evil for evil. Provide things honest in the sight of all men.

18. If it be possible, as much as lieth in you live peaceably with all men.

19. Dearly beloved avenge not yourselves, but rather give place unto wrath: for it is written, Vengeance is mine; I will repay, saith the Lord.

20. Therefore if thine enemy hunger, feed him; if he thirst, give him drink: for in so doing thou shalt heap coals of fire on his head.

21. Be not overcome of evil, but overcome evil with good.

EXODUS 20:2. I am The Lord thy God, which have brought thee out of the land of Egypt, out of the house of bondage.

3. Thou shalt have no other Gods before me.

EXODUS 22:20. He that sacrificed unto any God, save unto The Lord only, he shall be utterly destroyed.

EXODUS 34:14. For thou shalt worship no other God: for The Lord, whose name is Jealous, is a jealous God;

DEUTERONOMY 13:1. If there arise among you a prophet, or a dreamer of dreams, and giveth thee a sign or a wonder,

2. And the sign or the wonder come to pass, whereof he speak unto thee, saying, Let us go after other gods, which thou hast not known, and let us serve them;

3. THOU SHALT NOT hearken unto the words of that prophet, or that dreamer of dreams: for The Lord your God proveth you, to know whether ye love The Lord your God with all your heart and with all your soul.

4. Ye shall walk after the Lord your God, and fear him, and keep his commandments, and obey his voice, and ye shall serve him, and cleave unto him.

5. And that prophet, or that dreamer of dreams, shall be put to

death, because he hath spoken to turn you away from The Lord your God, which brought you out of the land of Egypt, and redeemed you out of the house of bondage, to thrust thee aside out of the way which The Lord thy God commanded thee to walk in. So shalt thou put the evil away from the midst of thee?

6. If thy brother, the son of thy mother, or thy son, or thy daughter, or the wife of thy bosom, or thy friend that is as thine own soul, entice thee secretly, saying, Let us go and serve other gods, which thou hast not known, thou, nor thy fathers;

7. Namely, the gods of the people which are round about you, nigh unto thee, or far off from thee, from the one end of the earth even unto the other end of the earth;

8. THOU SHALT NOT consent unto him, nor hearken unto him; neither shall thine eye pity him, neither shalt thou spare, neither shalt thou conceal him.

MATTHEW 6:24. No man can serve two masters; for either he will hate the one, and love the other; or else he will hold to the one, and despise the other. Ye cannot serve God and mammon.

(Mammon - wealth; worldly gain. Greed for riches; cupidity) (cupidity- an eager desire for possession, especially for wealth; covetousness; miserliness)

EXODUS 20:4. THOU SHALT NOT make unto thee a given image, nor any likeness of any thing that is in heaven above, or that is in the earth beneath, or that is in the water under the earth:

EXODUS 20:5. THOU SHALT NOT bow down thyself to them, nor serve them; for I THE LORD thy God am a jealous god, visiting the iniquity of the fathers upon the children, upon the third, and upon the fourth generations of them that hate me;

EXODUS 34:17. THOU SHALT make thee no molten gods.

LEVITICUS 26:1. Ye shall make you no idols, neither shall ye rear you up a graven image, or a pillar, neither shall ye place any figured stone in your land, to bow down unto it: FOR I AM THE LORD YOUR GOD.

DEUTERONOMY 27:15. Cursed be the man that maketh a graven or molten image, an abomination unto THE LORD, the work of the hands of the craftsman, and seteth it in a secret place.

EXODUS 20:7. THOU SHALT NOT take the name of THE LORD thy

God in vain; for THE LORD will not hold him guiltless that taketh him name in vain.

LEVITICUS 19:12. And ye shall not swear by my name falsely, and profane the name of thy God: I AM THE LORD.

MATTHEW 5:33. Again, ye have heard that it hath been said by them of old time, THOU SHALT NOT forswear thyself, but shalt perform unto The Lord thine oaths:

34. But I say unto you, Swear not at all; neither by heaven; for it is God's throne:

35. Nor by the earth; for it is his footstool: neither by Jerusalem; for it is the city of the great King.

36. Neither shalt thou swear by thy head, because thou canst not make one hair white or black.

37. But let your communication be, Yea, yea, Nay, nay; for whatsoever is more than these cometh of evil.

EXODUS 20:8. REMEMBER THE SABBATH DAY TO KEEP IT HOLY.

9. Six days shalt thou labour, and do all thy work:

10. But the seventh day is the Sabbath of The Lord thy God: in it THOU SHALT NOT do any work, thou, nor thy son, nor thy daughter, thy manservant, nor thy maidservant, nor thy cattle, nor thy stranger that is within thy gates:

11. For in six days The Lord made heaven and earth, the sea, and all that in them is, and rested the seventh day: wherefore The Lord blessed the Sabbath day, and hallowed it.

GENESIS 2:2. And on the seventh day God ended his work which he had made; and he rested on the seventh day from all his work which he had made.

3. And God blessed the seventh day, and sanctified it: because that in it he had rested from all his work which God created and made.

EXODUS 12:16. ...and in the seventh day there shall be a holy convocation to you; no manner of work shall be done in them, save that which every man must eat, that only may be done of you.

EXODUS 16:28. And The Lord said unto Moses, How long refuse ye to keep my commandments and my laws?

29. See, for that The Lord hath given you the Sabbath, therefore he giveth you on the sixth day the bread of two days; abide ye every man in his place, let no man go out of his place on the seventh day.

EXODUS 35:2. Six days shall work be done, but on the seventh day there shall be to you an holy day, a Sabbath of rest to the Lord: whosoever doeth work therein shall be put to death.

3. Ye shall kindle no fire throughout your habitations upon the Sabbath day.

LEVITICUS 19:3. Ye shall fear every man his mother, and his father, and keep my Sabbaths: I am The Lord your God.

26:2. Ye shall keep my Sabbaths, and reverence my sanctuary: I am The Lord.

NEHEMIAH 10:31. And if the peoples of the land bring ware or any victuals on the Sabbath day to sell, that we would not buy it of them on the Sabbath, or on a holy day.

ISAIAH 56:2. Blessed is the man that doeth this, and the son of man that layeth hold on it; that keepeth the Sabbath from polluting it, and keepeth his hand from doing any evil.

ISAIAH 58:13. If thou turn away thy foot from the Sabbath, from doing thy pleasure on my holy day; and call the Sabbath a delight, and the holy of The Lord honourable; and shalt honour him, not doing thine own ways, nor finding thine own pleasure, nor speaking thine own words:

14. Then shalt thou delight thyself in The Lord; and I will cause thee to ride upon the high places of the earth; and I will feed thee with the heritage of Jacob thy father: FOR THE MOUTH OF THE LORD HATH SPOKEN IT.

JEREMIAH 17:21. Thus saith The Lord; Take heed to yourselves, and bear no burden on the Sabbath day, nor bring it in by the gates of Jerusalem;

22. Neither carry forth a burden out of your houses on the Sabbath day, neither do ye any work, but hallow ye the Sabbath day, as I commanded your fathers.

MARK 2:27. And he said unto them, the Sabbath was made for man, and not man for the Sabbath:

28. Therefore the Son of man is Lord even of the Sabbath.

LUKE 13:14. And the ruler of the synagogue, answered with indignation, because Jesus had healed on the Sabbath day and said unto the people, There are six days in which men ought to work: in them therefore come and be healed, and not on the Sabbath day.

16. And ought not this woman, being a daughter of Abraham, whom Satan hath bound, lo, these eighteen years to have been loosed from this bond on the Sabbath day?

EXODUS 20:12. HONOUR THY FATHER AND THY MOTHER: that thy days may be long upon the land which The Lord thy God giveth thee:

EXODUS 21:15. And he that smiteth his father, or his mother, shall be surely put to death.

17. And he that curseth his father, or his mother, shall surely be put to death.

LEVITICUS 20:9. For every one that curseth his father, or his mother, shall surely be put to death: he hath cursed his father or his mother: his blood shall be upon him.

DEUTERONOMY 27:16. Cursed be he that setteth light by his father or his mother.

EXODUS 20:13. THOU SHALT NOT KILL

EXODUS 21:12. He that smiteth a man, so that he dieth, shall be surely put to death.

13. And if a man lie not in wait, but God deliver him into his hand; then I will appoint thee a place whither he shall flee.

14. But if a man come presumptuously upon his neighbour, to slay him with guile; thou shalt take him from mine altar that he may die.

NUMBERS 35:16. And if he smite him with an instrument of iron, so that he die, he is a murderer: the murderer shall surely be put to death.

17. And if he smite him with throwing a stone, wherewith he may die, and he die, he is a murderer: the murderer shall surely be put to death.

18. Or if he smites him with an hand weapon of wood, wherewith he may die, and he dies, he is a murderer: the murderer shall surely be put to death.

30. Whoso killeth any person, the murderer shall be put to death by the mouth of witnesses: but one witness shall not testify against any person to cause him to die.

31. Moreover ye shall take no satisfaction for the life of a murderer, which is guilty of death: but he shall be surely put to death.

MATTHEW 5:21. Ye have heard that it was said by them of old time,

THOU SHALT NOT KILL; and whosoever shall kill shall be in danger of the judgment:

22. But I say unto you, that whosoever is angry with his brother without a cause shall be in danger of the judgment: and whosoever shall say to his brother, Raca, shall be in danger of the council: but whosoever shall say, Thou fool, shall be in danger of hellfire.

GALATIANS 5:21. Envyings, murders, drunkenness, revellings, and such like: of the which I tell you before, as I have also told you in time past, that they which do such things shall not inherit the kingdom of God.

REVELATION 21:8. But the fearful, and unbelieving, and the abominable, and murderers, and whoremongers, and sorcerers, and idolaters, and all liars, shall have their part in the lake which burneth with fire and brimstone: which is the second death.

REVELATION 22:14. Blessed are they that do his commandments that they may have right to the tree of life, and may enter in through the gates into the city.

15. For without are dogs, and sorcerers, and whoremongers, and murderers, and idolaters, and whosoever loveth and maketh a lie.

I TIMOTHY 1:8. But we know that the law is good, if a man use it lawfully;

9. Knowing this, that the law is not made for a righteous man, but for the lawless and disobedient, for the ungodly and for sinners, for unholy and profane, for murderers of fathers and murderers of mothers, for manslayers.

MATTHEW 26:52. Then Jesus said unto him, Put up again thy sword into his place: for all they that take the sword shall perish with the sword.

EXODUS 20:14. THOU SHALT NOT commit adultery.

LEVITICUS 18:20. Moreover thou shalt not lie carnally with thy neighbor's wife, to defile thyself with her.

LEVITICUS 20:10. And the man that committeth adultery with another man's wife, even he that committeth adultery with his neighbour's wife, the adulterer and the adulteress shall surely be put to death.

DEUTERONOMY 22:22. If a man be found lying with a woman married to a husband, then they shall both of them die, both the man that lay with the woman, and the woman;

PROVERBS 6:26. For by means of a whorish woman a man is brought to a piece of bread: and the adulteress will hunt for the precious life.

27. Can a man take fire in his bosom and his clothes not be burned?

28. Can one go upon hot coals, and his feet not be burned?

29. So he that goeth in to his neighbour's wife; whosoever toucheth her shall not be innocent.

32. But whoso committeth adultery with a woman lacketh understanding; he that doeth it destroyeth his own soul.

33. A wound and dishonor shall he get: and his reproach shall not be wiped away.

MATTHEW 5:27. Ye have heard that it was said by them of old time. Thou shalt not commit adultery:

28. But I say unto you, that whosoever looketh on a woman to lust after her hath committeth adultery with her already in his heart.

29. And if the right eye offend thee, pluck it out, and cast it from thee: for it is profitable for thee that one of thy members should perish, and not that thy whole body should be cast into hell.

30. And if thy right hand offend thee cut it off, and cast it from thee: for it is profitable for thee that one of thy members should perish, and not that thy whole body should be cast into hell.

32. But I say unto you, that whosoever shall put away his wife, saving for the cause of fornication, causeth her to commit adultery: and whosoever shall marry her that is divorced committeth adultery.

II PETER 2:14. Having eyes full of adultery and that cannot cease from sin; beguiling unstable souls: An heart they have exercised with covetous practices; cursed children:

15. Which have forsaken the right way, and are gone astray,—who loved the wages of unrighteousness;

17. These are wells without water, clouds that are carried with a tempest; to whom the mist of darkness is reserved forever.

20. For if after they have escaped the pollutions of the world through the knowledge of the Lord and Saviour Jesus Christ, they are again entangled therein, and overcome, the latter end is worse with them than the beginning.

21. For it had been better for them not to have known the way of righteousness, than, after they have known it, to turn from the holy commandment delivered unto them.

EXODUS 20:15. THOU SHALT NOT STEAL.

LEVITICUS 19:11. Ye shall not steal, neither deal falsely, neither lie one to another.

13. Thou shalt not defraud thy neighbour, neither rob him:

DEUTERONOMY 24:7. If a man be found stealing any of his brethren...and maketh merchandise of him, or selleth him, then that thief shall die; and thou shalt put evil away from among you.

JEREMIAH 23:30. Therefore, behold, I am against the prophets, saith the Lord, that steal my words every one from his neighbour.

MATTHEW 19:16. And, behold, one came and said unto him, Good Master, what good thing shall I do, that I may have eternal life?

17. And he said unto him, Why callest thou me good? There is none good but one, that is, God: but if thou wilt enter into life, keep the commandments.

18. He saith unto him, which? Jesus said, Thou shalt do no murder, Thou shalt not commit adultery, Thou shalt not steal, Thou shalt not bear false witness,

19. Honor thy father and thy mother: and, Thou shalt love thy neighbour as thyself.

EPHESIANS 4:28. Let him that stole steal no more: but rather let him labour, working with his hands the thing which is good, that he may have to give to him that needeth.

EXODUS 20:16. THOU SHALT NOT bear false witness against thy neighbour.

EXODUS 23:1. THOU SHALT NOT raise a false report: put not thine hand with the wicked to be an unrighteous witness.

LEVITICUS 19:16. THOU SHALT NOT go up and down as a talebearer among thy people; NEITHER SHALT THOU stand against the blood of thy neighbour: I AM THE LORD.

EXODUS 20:17. THOU SHALT NOT covet thy neighbour's house; THOU SHALT NOT covet thy neighbour's wife, nor his manservant, nor his maidservant, nor his ox, nor his ass, nor any thing that is thy neighbour's.

MICAH 2:1. Woe to them that devise iniquity, and work evil upon their beds: when the morning is light, they practice it, because it is in the power of their hand.

2. And they covet fields, and take them by violence, and houses, and take them away: so they oppress a man and his house, even a man and his heritage.

3. Therefore thus saith the Lord, Behold, against this family do I devise an evil, from which ye shall not remove your necks; neither shall ye go haughtily: for this time is evil.

EPHESIANS 5:5. For this ye know, that no whoremonger, nor unclean person, nor covetous man, who is an idolater, hath any inheritance in the kingdom of Christ and of God.

EXODUS 22:18. THOU SHALT NOT SUFFER A WITCH TO LIVE.

LEVITICUS 20:27. A man also or a woman that hath a familiar spirit, or that is a wizard, shall surely be put to death: they shall stone them with stones: their blood shall be upon them.

LEVITICUS 19:31. Regard not them that have familiar spirits, neither seek after wizards, to be defiled by them: I AM THE LORD YOUR GOD.

LEVITICUS 20:6. And the soul that turneth after such as have familiar spirits, and after wizards to go a-whoring after them, I will even set my face against that soul, and will cut him off from among his people.

EXODUS 22:21. THOU SHALT NEITHER vex a stranger nor oppress him:

LEVITICUS 19:33. And if a stranger sojourn with thee in your land, ye shall not vex him.

34. But the stranger that dwelleth with you shall be unto you as one born among you, and thou shalt love him as thyself...I AM THE LORD YOUR GOD.

DEUTERONOMY 27:19. Cursed be he that perverted the judgment of the stranger, fatherless, and widow.

EXODUS 22:22. YE SHALL NOT afflict any widow, or fatherless child.

EXODUS 22:23. If thou afflict them in any wise, and they cry at all unto me, I will surely hear their cry.

24. And my wrath shall wax hot, and I will kill you with the sword; and

your wives shall be widows, and your children fatherless.

EXODUS 22:25. If thou lend money to any of my people that are poor by thee, THOU SHALT NOT be to him as a usurer, neither shall thou lay upon him usury.

LEVITICUS 25:35. And if thy brother be waxen poor, and fallen in decay with thee; then thou shalt relieve him: yea, though he be a stranger, or a sojourner; that he may live with thee.

36. Take thou no usury of him, or increase; but fear thy God; that thy brother may live with thee.

37. THOU SHALT NOT give him thy money upon usury, nor lend him thy victuals for increase.

DEUTERONOMY 23:19. THOU SHALT NOT lend upon usury to thy brother, usury of money, usury of victuals, and usury of any thing that is lent upon usury.

20. Unto a stranger thou mayest lend upon usury;

EXODUS 22:28. THOU SHALT NOT revile the gods, nor curse the ruler of thy people.

29. THOU SHALT NOT delay to offer the first of thy ripe fruits, and of thy liquors: the firstborn of thy sons shalt thou give unto me.

31. And ye shall be holy men unto me: neither shall ye eat any flesh that is torn of beasts in the field; ye shall cast it to the dogs.

LEVITICUS 22:8. That which dieth of itself, or is torn with beasts, he shall not eat to defile himself therewith: I AM THE LORD.

EXODUS 23:2. THOU SHALT NOT follow a multitude to do evil; neither shalt thou speak in a cause to decline after many to wrest judgment:

3. Neither shalt thou countenance a poor man in his cause.

4. If thou meet thine enemy's ox or his ass going astray, thou shalt surely bring it back to him again.

5. If thou see the ass of him that hateth thee lying under his burden, and wouldest forbear to help him, thou shalt surely help with him.

6. THOU SHALT NOT wrest the judgment of thy poor in his cause.

7. Keep thee far from a false matter; and the innocent and righteous slay thou not: for I will not justify the wicked.

8. And thou shalt take no gifts: for the gift blindeth the wise, and perverteth the words of the righteous.

9. Also THOU SHALT NOT oppress a stranger:

LEVITICUS 18:6. None of you shall approach to any that is near of kin to him, to uncover their nakedness: I AM THE LORD.

7. The nakedness of thy father, or the nakedness of thy mother, SHALT THOU NOT uncover: she is thy mother; THOU SHALT NOT uncover her nakedness.

8. The nakedness of thy father's wife SHALT THOU NOT uncover; it is thy father's nakedness.

LEVITICUS 20:11. And the man that lieth with his father's wife hath uncovered his father's nakedness: both of them shall surely be put to death; their blood shall be upon them.

I CORINTHIANS 5:1. It is reported commonly that there is fornication among you, and such fornication as is not so much as named among the Gentiles, that one should have his father's wife.

2. And ye are puffed up, and have not rather mourned; that he that hath done this deed might be taken away from among you.

5. To deliver such an one unto Satan for the destruction of the flesh, that the spirit may be saved in the day of the Lord Jesus.

LEVITICUS 18:9. The nakedness of thy sister, the daughter of thy father, or the daughter of thy mother, whether she be born at home, or born abroad, even their nakedness THOU SHALT NOT uncover.

11. The nakedness of thy father's wife's daughter, begotten of thy father, she is thy sister; THOU SHALT NOT uncover her nakedness.

LEVITICUS 20:17. And if a man shall take his sister, his father's daughter, or his mother's daughter, and see her nakedness, and she see his nakedness; it is a wicked thing; and they shall be cut off in the sight of their people; he hath uncovered his sister's nakedness; he shall bear his iniquity.

DEUTERONOMY 27:22. Cursed be he that lieth with his sister, the daughter of his father, or the daughter of his mother.

LEVITICUS 18:10. The nakedness of thy son's daughter, or of thy daughter's daughter, even their nakedness THOU SHALT NOT uncover: for theirs is thine own nakedness.

LEVITICUS 18:12. THOU SHALT NOT uncover the nakedness of thy father's sister: she is thy father's near kinswoman.

13. THOU SHALT NOT uncover the nakedness of thy mother's sister: for she is thy mother's near kinswoman.

LEVITICUS 20:19. And THOU SHALT NOT uncover the nakedness of thy mother's sister, nor thy father's sister; for he uncovereth his near kin: they shall bear their iniquity.

LEVITICUS 18:14. THOU SHALT NOT uncover the nakedness of thy father's brother, THOU SHALT NOT approach to his wife: she is thine aunt.

LEVITICUS 20:20. And if a man shall lie with his uncle's wife, he hath uncovered his uncle's nakedness; they shall bear their sin; they shall die childless.

LEVITICUS 18:15. THOU SHALT NOT uncover the nakedness of thy daughter in law: she is thy son's wife; THOU SHALT NOT uncover her nakedness.

LEVITICUS 20:12. And if a man lie with his daughter in law, both of them shall surely be put to death: they have wrought confusion; their blood shall be upon them.

LEVITICUS 18:16. THOU SHALT NOT uncover the nakedness of thy brother's wife: it is thy brother's nakedness.

LEVITICUS 20:21. And if a man shall take his brother's wife. It is an unclean thing: he hath uncovered his brother's nakedness; they shall be childless.

LEVITICUS 18:17. THOU SHALT NOT uncover the nakedness of a woman and her daughter, neither shalt thou take her son's daughter, or her daughter's daughter, to uncover her nakedness; for they are her near kinswomen; it is wickedness.

LEVITICUS 20:14. And if a man takes a wife and her mother, it is wickedness: they shall be burnt with fire, both he and they; that there is no wickedness among you.

DEUTERONOMY 27:23. Cursed be he that lieth with his mother in law.

LEVITICUS 18:18. NEITHER SHALT THOU take a wife to her sister, to vex her, to uncover her nakedness, beside the other in her life time.

19. Also THOU SHALT NOT approach unto a woman to uncover her nakedness, as long as she is put apart for her uncleanness.

LEVITICUS 20:18. And if a man shall lie with a woman having her sickness, and shall uncover her nakedness; he hath discovered her fountain, and she hath uncovered the fountain of her blood: and both of them shall be cut off from among their people.

LEVITICUS 18:21. THOU SHALT NOT let any of thy seed pass through the fire to Molech; neither shalt thou profane the name of thy God: I AM THE LORD.

(MOLECH - the fire god of the ancient Phoenicians and Ammonites, worshiped by human sacrifice).

LEVITICUS 18:22. THOU SHALT NOT lie with mankind, as with womankind; it is abomination.

LEVITICUS 20:13. If a man also lie with mankind, as he lieth with a woman, both of them have committed an abomination: they shall surely be put to death; their blood shall be upon them.

LEVITICUS 18:23. NEITHER SHALL THOU lie with any beast to defile thyself therewith: neither shall any woman stand before a beast to lie down thereto; it is confusion.

EXODUS 22:19. Whosoever lieth with a beast shall surely be put to death.

LEVITICUS 20:15. And if a man lie with a beast, he shall surely be put to death: and ye shall slay the beast.

16. And if a woman approach unto a beast, and lie down thereto, thou shall kill the woman, and the beast: they shall surely be put to death; there blood shall be upon them.

LEVITICUS 18:24. Defile not ye yourselves in any of these things: for in all these the nations are defiled which I cast out before you:

25. And the land is defiled; therefore I do visit the iniquity thereof upon it, and the land itself vomiteth out her inhabitants.

26. Ye shall therefore keep my statutes and my judgments, and shall not commit any of these abominations; neither any of your own nation, nor any stranger that sojourneth among you:

28. That the land spued not you out also, when ye defile it, as it spued out the nations that were before you.

30...I AM THE LORD YOUR GOD.

LEVITICUS 19:9. And when ye reap the harvest of your land, THOU

SHALT NOT wholly reap the corners of thy field, NEITHER SHALT THOU gather the gleanings of thy harvest.

10. And THOU SHALT NOT glean thy vineyard, NEITHER SHALT THOU gather every grape of thy vineyard; thou shalt leave them for the poor and stranger: I AM THE LORD YOUR GOD.

14. THOU SHALT NOT curse the deaf, nor put a stumbling block before the blind, but shall fear thy God: I AM THE LORD.

15. YE SHALL DO NO unrighteousness in judgment: THOU SHALT NOT respect the person of the poor, not honour the person of the mighty: but in righteousness shalt thou judge thy neighbor.

19. Ye shall keep my statutes, THOU SHALT NOT let thy cattle gender with a diverse kind: THOU SHALT NOT sow thy field with mingled seed: NEITHER SHALL a garment mingled of linen and woolen come upon thee.

DEUTERONOMY 22:9. THOU SHALT NOT sow thy vineyard with divers' seeds: lest the fruit of thy seed which thou hast sown, and the fruit of thy vineyard, be defiled.

11. THOU SHALT NOT wear a garment of divers' sorts, as of woolen and linen together.

LEVITICUS 19:26. YE SHALL NOT eat any thing with the blood: NEITHER SHALL YE use enchantment, nor observe times.

LEVITICUS 7:26. Moreover ye shall eat no manner of blood, whether it is of fowl or of beast, in any of your dwellings.

27. Whatsoever soul it is that eateth any manner of blood, even that soul shall be cut off from his people.

LEVITICUS 17:11. For the life of the flesh is in the blood: and I have given it to you upon the altar to make atonement for your souls: for it is the blood that maketh atonement for the soul.

DEUTERONOMY 12:23. Only be sure that thou eat not the blood: for the blood is the life and thou mayest not eat the life with the flesh.

25. THOU SHALT NOT eat it; that it may go well with thee and with thy children after thee, when thou shalt do that which is right in the sight of the Lord.

32. What thing so ever I command you, observe to do it: THOU SHALT NOT add thereto, nor diminish from it.

LEVITICUS 19:35. YE SHALL DO NO unrighteousness in judgment, in meteyard, in weight, or in measure.

36. Just balances, just weights, a just ephah, and a just hin, shall ye have: I AM THE LORD YOUR GOD.

LEVITICUS 25:17. YE SHALL NOT therefore oppress one another; but thou shalt fear thy God: FOR I AM THE LORD YOUR GOD.

DEUTERONOMY 1:17. YE SHALL NOT respect persons in judgment; but ye shall hear the small as well as the great; YE SHALL NOT is afraid of the face of man; for the judgment is God's:

DEUTERONOMY 22:1. THOU SHALT NOT see thy brother's ox or his sheep go astray, and hide thyself from them: thou shalt in any case bring them again unto thy brother.

2. And if thy brother be not nigh unto thee, or if thou know him not, then thou shalt bring it unto thine own house, and it shall be with thee until thy brother seek after it, and thou shalt restore it to him again.

3. In like manner shalt thou do with his ass; and so shall thou do with his raiment; and with all lost thing of thy brother's, which he hath lost, and thou hast found, shalt thou do likewise: thou mayest not hide thyself.

4. THOU SHALT NOT see thy brother's ass or his ox fall down by the way, and hide thyself from them: thou shalt surely help him to lift them up again.

5. The woman shall not wear that which pertaineth unto a man; neither shall a man put on a woman's garment: for all that do so are abomination unto the Lord thy God.

DEUTERONOMY 23:7. THOU SHALT NOT abhor an Edomite; for he is thy brother: THOU SHALT NOT abhor an Egyptian; because thou wast a stranger in his land.

18. THOU SHALT NOT bring the hire of a whore, or the price of a dog, into the house of the Lord thy God for any vow: for even both these are abominations unto the Lord thy God.

21. When thou shalt vow a vow unto the Lord thy God, THOU SHALT NOT slack to pay it: for the Lord thy God will surely require it of thee; and it would be sin in thee.

23. That which is gone out of thy lips thou shalt keep and perform; even a freewill offering, according as thou hast vowed unto the Lord thy God, which thou hast promised with thy mouth.

24. When thou comest into thy neighbour's vineyard, then thou mayest eat grapes thy fill at thine own pleasure; but THOU SHALT NOT put any in thy vessel.

25. When thou comest into the standing corn of thy neighbour, then thou mayest pluck the ears with thine hand; but THOU SHALT NOT move

a sickle unto thy neighbour's standing corn.

DEUTERONOMY 24:1. When a man hath taken a wife, and married her, and it come to pass that she find no favor in his eyes, because he hath found some uncleanness in her: then let him write her a bill of divorcement, and give it in her hand, and send her out of his house.

2. And when she is departed out of his house, she may go and be another man's wife.

3. And if the latter husband hate her, and write her a bill of divorcement, and giveth it in her hand, and sendeth her out of his house; or if the latter husband die, which took her to be his wife.

4. Her former husband, which sent her away, may not take her again to be his wife, after that she is defiled; for that is abomination before the Lord: and THOU SHALT NOT cause the land to sin, which the Lord thy God giveth thee for a inheritance.

DEUTERONOMY 24:14. THOU SHALT NOT oppress a hired servant that is poor and needy, whether he be of thy brethren, or of thy strangers that are in thy land within thy gates:

17. THOU SHALT NOT pervert the judgment of the stranger, nor of the fatherless, nor take a widow's raiment to pledge:

DEUTERONOMY 25:4. THOU SHALT NOT muzzle the ox when he treadeth out the corn.

13. THOU SHALT NOT have in thy bag divers' measures, a great and a small.

14. THOU SHALT NOT have in thine house divers' measures, a great and a small.

15. But thou shalt have a perfect and just weight, a perfect and just measure shalt thou have: that thy days may be lengthened in the land which the Lord thy God giveth thee.

FOOD LAWS

LEVITICUS 20:25. Ye shall therefore put difference between clean beasts and unclean, and between unclean fowls and clean: and YE SHALL NOT make your souls abominable by beasts, or by fowl, or by any manner of living thing that creepeth on the ground, which I have separated from you as unclean.

DEUTERONOMY 14:3. THOU SHALT NOT eat any abominable thing.

4. These are the beasts which ye shall eat: the ox, the sheep, and the goat.

5. The hart, and the roebuck, and the fallow deer, and the wild goat,

and the pygarg, and the wild ox, and the chamois.

6. And every beast that parteth the hoof, and cleaveth the cleft into two claws, and cheweth the cud among the beasts, that ye shall eat.

7. Nevertheless these ye shall not eat of them that chew the cud, or of them that divide the cloven hoof; as the camel, and the hare, and the coney: for they chew the cud, but divide not the hoof; therefore they are unclean unto you.

8. And the swine, because it divideth the hoof, yet cheweth not the cud, it is unclean unto you: ye shall not eat of their flesh, nor touch their dead carcass.

9. These ye shall eat of all that are in the waters: all that have fins and scales shall ye eat:

10. And whatsoever hath not fins and scales ye may not eat; it is unclean unto you.

11. Of all clean birds ye shall eat.

12. But these are they of which ye shall not eat: the eagle, and the ossifrage, and the osprey,

13. And the glede, and the kite, and the vulture after his kind.

14. And every raven after his kind.

15. And the owl, and the night hawk, and the cuckoo, and the hawk after his kind.

16. The little owl, and the great owl, and the swan.

17. And the pelican, and the gier eagle, and the cormorant.

18. And the stork, and the heron after her kind, and the lapwing, and the bat.

19. And every creeping thing that flieth is unclean unto you: they shall not be eaten.

20. But of all clean fowls ye may eat.

21. Ye shall not eat of any thing that dieth of itself: thou shalt give it unto the stranger that is in thy gates, that he may eat it; or thou mayest sell it unto an alien: for thou art an holy people unto the Lord thy God. THOU SHALT NOT seethe a kid in his mother's milk.

PROMISED BLESSINGS

LEVITICUS 26:3. If ye walk in my statutes, and keep my commandments, and do them;

4. Then I will give you rain in due season, and the land shall yield her increase, and the trees of the field shall yield their fruit.

5. And your threshing shall reach unto the vintage, and the vintage shall reach unto the sowing time; and ye shall eat your bread to the full, and dwell in your land safely.

9. For I will have respect unto you, and make you fruitful, and multiply you, and establish my covenant with you.

10. And ye shall eat old store, and bring forth the old because of the new.

11. And I will set my tabernacle among you: and my soul shall not abhor you.

12. And I will walk among you, and will be your God, and ye shall be my people.

DEUTERONOMY 28:9. The Lord shall establish thee an holy people unto himself, as he hath sworn unto thee, if thou shalt keep the commandments of the Lord thy God, and walk in his ways.

10. And all people of the earth shall see that thou art called by the name of the Lord; and they shall be afraid of thee.

12. ...and thou shalt lend unto many nations, and thou shalt not borrow.

13. And the Lord shall make thee the head, and not the tail...if that thou hearken unto the commandments of the Lord thy God...to observe and to do them:

14. And thou shalt not go aside from any of the words which I command thee this day, to the right hand, or to the left, to go after other gods to serve them.

PROMISED PUNISHMENTS

LEVITICUS 26:14. But if ye will not hearken unto me, and will not do all these commandments;

15. And if ye shall despise my statutes, or if your soul abhor my judgments, so that ye will not do all my commandments, but that ye break my covenant;

16. I also will do this unto you; I will even appoint over you terror, consumption, and the burning ague, that shall consume the eyes, and cause sorrow of heart: and ye shall sow your seed in vain, for your enemies shall eat it.

17. And I will set my face against you, and ye shall be slain before your enemies: they that hate you shall reign over you; and ye shall flee when none pursueth you.

18. And if ye will not yet for all this hearken unto me, then I will punish you seven times more for your sins.

19. And I will break the pride of your power; and I will make your heaven as iron, and your earth as brass:

20. And your strength shall be spent in vain: for your land shall not yield her increase, neither shall the trees of the land yield their fruits.

21. And if ye walk contrary unto me, and will not hearken unto me; I will bring seven times more plagues upon you according to your sins.

22. I will also send wild beasts among you, which shall rob you of your

children, and destroy your cattle, and make you few in number; and your high ways shall be desolate.

23. And if ye will not be reformed by me by these things, but will walk contrary unto me;

24. Then will I also walk contrary unto you, and will punish you yet seven times for your sins.

25. And I will bring a sword upon you that shall avenge the quarrel of my covenant: and when ye are gathered together within your cities, I will send the pestilence among you: and ye shall be delivered into the hand of the enemy.

26. And when I have broken the staff of your bread, ten women shall bake your bread in one oven, and they shall deliver you your bread again by weight: and ye shall eat, and not be satisfied.

27. And if ye will not for all this hearken unto me, but walk contrary unto me;

28. Then I will walk contrary unto you also in fury; and I, even I, will chastise you seven times for your sins.

29. And ye shall eat the flesh of your sons, and the flesh of your daughters shall ye eat.

30. And I will destroy your high places, and cut down your images, and cast your carcasses upon the carcasses of your idols, and my soul shall abhor you.

31. And I will make your cities waste, and bring your sanctuaries unto desolation, and I will not smell the saviour of your sweet odours.

33. And I will scatter you among the heathen, and will draw out a sword after you:

36. And upon them that are left alive of you I will send a faintness into their hearts in the lands of their enemies; and the sound of a shaken leaf shall shake them; and they shall flee, as fleeing from a sword; and they shall fall when none pursueth.

37. And they shall fall one upon another, as it were before a sword, when none pursueth: and ye shall have no power to stand before your enemies.

38. And ye shall perish among the heathen, and the land of your enemies shall eat you up.

39. And they that are left of you shall pine away in their iniquity in your enemies' lands; and also in the iniquities of their father's shall they pine away with them.

40. If they shall confess their iniquity, and the iniquity of their fathers, with their trespass which they trespassed against me, and that also they have walked contrary unto me;

41. And that I also have walked contrary unto them, and have brought them into the land of their enemies; if then their uncircumcised hearts be

humbled, and they then accept of the punishment of their iniquity:

42. Then will I remember my covenant.........

43. ....because, even because they despised my judgments, and because their soul abhorred my statutes.

44. And yet for all that, when they be in the land of their enemies, I will not cast them away, neither will I abhor them, to destroy them utterly, and to break my covenant with them: for I AM THE LORD THEIR GOD.

DEUTERONOMY 28:43. The stranger that is within thee shall get up above thee very high; and thou shalt come down very low.

44. He shall lend to thee, and thou shalt not lend to him: he shall be the head, and thou shalt be the tail.

45. Moreover all these curses shall come upon thee, and shall pursue thee, and overtake thee, till thou be destroyed; because thou hearkenedst not unto the voice of the Lord thy God, to keep his commandments and his statutes which he commanded thee.

46. And they shall be upon thee for a sign and for a wonder, and upon thy seed for ever.

47. Because thou servedst not the Lord thy God with joyfulness, and with gladness of heart, for the abundance of all things.

48. Therefore shalt thou serve thine enemies which the Lord shall send against thee, in hunger, and in thirst, and in nakedness, and in want of all things: and he shall put a yoke of iron upon thy neck, until he has destroyed thee.

49. The Lord shall bring a nation against thee from far, from the end of the earth, as swift as the eagle flieth; a nation whose tongue thou shalt not understand;

50. A nation of fierce countenance, which shall not regard the person of the old, nor shew favour to the young:

51. And he shall eat the fruit of thy cattle, and the fruit of thy land, until thou be destroyed: which also shall not leave thee either corn, wine, or oil, or the increase of thy kine, of flocks of thy sheep, until he have destroyed thee.

52. And he shall besiege thee in all thy gates, until thy high and fenced walls come down, wherein thou trustedst, throughout all thy land: and he shall besiege thee in all thy gates throughout all thy land, which the Lord thy God hath given thee.

53. And thou shalt eat the fruit of thine own body, the flesh of thy sons and of thy daughters, which the Lord thy God hath given thee, in the siege, and in the straitness wherewith thine enemies shall distress thee:

54. So that the man that is tender among you, and very delicate, his eye shall be evil toward his brother, and toward the wife of his bosom, and

toward the remnant of his children which he shall leave:

55. So that he will not give to any of them of the flesh of his children whom he shall eat: because he hath nothing left him in the siege, and in the straitness, wherewith thine enemies shall distress thee in all thy gates.

56. The tender and delicate woman among you, who would not adventure to set the sole of her foot upon the ground for delicateness and tenderness, her eye shall be evil toward the husband of her bosom, and toward her son, and toward her daughter.

57. And toward her young one that cometh out from between her feet, and toward her children which she shall bear: for she shall eat them for want of all things secretly in the siege and straitness, wherewith thine enemy shall distress thee in thy gates.

58. If thou wilt not observe to do all the words of this law that are written in this book, that thou mayest fear this glorious and fearful name, THE LORD THY GOD;

59. Then the Lord will make the plagues wonderful, and the plagues of thy seed, even great plagues, and of long continuance, and sore sicknesses, and of long continuance.

61. Also every sickness, and every plague, which is not written in the book of this law, them will the Lord bring upon thee, until thou be destroyed.

63. And it shall come to pass, that as the Lord rejoiced over you to do you good, and to multiply you; so the Lord will rejoice over you to destroy you, and to bring you to nought; and ye shall be plucked from off the land……

ECCLESIASTES 12:13. Let us hear the conclusion of the whole matter; Fear God, and keep his commandments; for this is the whole duty of man.

BOOK IV

There are millions of people all over the world who have not even seen a Bible, let alone know of its contents. YES, EVEN HERE IN THE UNITED STATES. And there are millions who have seen it, yet have not read it. There are also millions who have read it, and do not understand what they have read. And there are millions who have read it, understand, but are 'Too busy going to and fro with their every day living,' as God has spoken to me, 'and are not being mindful of what they have read, nor of him.'

The Bible is full of instructions, admonitions, and etc., from Genesis to Revelation. This book will only contain what God has directed me to put into it at this time to be reviewed at one's leisure, or to be studied for one's salvation.

I would suggest that you have your Bible nearby for further studying and/or reading, if you so desire. As I have touched only a very small portion of those instructions, admonitions, and etc. Hopefully, this book will inspire you to want to know more of them. "My people are destroyed for lack of knowledge..." Hosea 5:6.

Will our lack of the knowledge of them or our disobedience to them keep us from going to heaven? I do not know. They may, since it was he who inspired me to write about them, and gave me the title. Yes, again they may. Let us not take that chance. Let us not 'let the little foxes spoil the vines.' (Cant. 2:15) DEUTEROMONY 12:32. WHAT THING SOEVER I COMMAND YOU, OBSERVE TO DO IT: THOU SHALL NOT ADD THERETO, NOR DIMINISH FROM IT.

I SAMUEL 15:22. And Samuel said, Hath the Lord as great delight in burnt offerings and sacrifices, as in obeying the voice of the Lord? Behold, to obey is better than sacrifice, and to hearken than the fat of rams.

23. For rebellion is as the sin of witchcraft, and stubbornness is as iniquity and idolatry. Because thou hast rejected the word of the Lord, he hath also rejected thee from being king.

EZEKIEL 3:17. Son of man, I have made thee a watchman unto the house of Israel: therefore hear the word at my mouth, and give them warning from me.

18. When I say unto the wicked, Thou shalt surely die; and thou givest him not warning, nor speakest to warn the wicked from his wicked way, to save his life; the same wicked man shall die in his iniquity; but his blood will I require at thine hand.

19. Yet if thou warn the wicked, and he turn not from his wickedness, nor from his wicked way, he shall die in his iniquity; but thou hast delivered thy soul.

20. Again, when a righteous man doth turn from his righteousness,

and commit iniquity, and I lay a stumbling block before him, he shall die: because thou hast not given him warning, he shall die in his sin, and his righteousness which he hath done shall not be remembered; but his blood will I require at thine hand.

21. Nevertheless if thou warn the righteous man, that the righteous sin not, and he doth not sin, he shall surely live, because he is warned; also thou hast delivered thy soul.

MALACHI 4:1. For, behold, the day cometh, that shall burn as an oven; and all the proud yea, and all that do wickedly, shall be stubble; and the day that cometh shall burn them up, saith the Lord of hosts, that it shall leave them neither root nor branch.

5. Behold, I will send you Elijah the prophet before the coming of the great and dreadful day of the Lord:

6. And he shall turn the heart of the fathers to the children, and the heart of the children to their fathers,

JOHN 1:1. In the beginning was the Word and the Word was with God, and the Word was God.

14. And the Word was made flesh, and dwelt among us...

16. And of his fullness have all we received and grace for grace.

17. For the law was given by Moses, but grace and truth came by Jesus Christ

29. ...the Lamb of God, which taketh away the sin of the world.

JOHN 3:5. ...Verily, verily, I say unto thee, except a man be born of water and of the spirit, he cannot enter into the kingdom of God.

14. And as Moses lifted up the serpent in the wilderness, even so must the Son of man be lifted up:

15. That whosoever believeth in him should not perish, but have eternal life.

17. For God sent not his Son into the World to condemn the world; but that the world through him might be saved.

LITTLE FOXES

"YE SHALL EAT NO BLOOD"

GENESIS 9:3. Every moving thing that liveth shall be meat for you;

4. But flesh with the life thereof, which is the blood thereof, shall ye not eat.

LEVITICUS 7:26. Moreover ye shall eat no manner of blood, whether it be of fowl or of beast...

LEVITICUS 17:11. For the life of the flesh is in the blood: and I have given it to you upon the altar to make atonement for your souls: for it is the blood that maketh atonement for the soul.

'YE SHALL EAT NO FAT"

LEVITICUS 3:16. ...all the fat is the Lord's.

17. It shall be a perpetual statute for your generations throughout all your dwellings, that ye eat neither fat nor blood.

LEVITICUS 7:22. And the Lord spoke unto Moses, saying,

23. ...ye shall eat no manner of fat, of ox, or of sheep, or of goat.

"HOLINESS" (moral and spiritual purity)

LEVITICUS 11:45. For I am Lord that bringeth you up out of the land of Egypt, to be your God: ye shall therefore be holy, for I am holy.

I CHRONICLE 16:29. ...worship the Lord in the beauty of holiness.

ISAIAH 35:8. And a highway shall be there, and a way, and it shall be called the way of holiness; the unclean shall not pass over it;

9. ...THE REDEEMED SHALL WALK THERE.

Romans 6:19. I speak after the manner of men because of the infirmity of your flesh: for as ye have yielded your members servants to uncleanness and to iniquity unto iniquity; even so now yield your members servants to righteousness unto holiness.

II CORINTHIANS 7:1. Having therefore these promises, dearly beloved, let us cleanse ourselves from all filthiness of the flesh and spirit, perfecting holiness in the fear of God.

"RIGHTEOUSNESS" (blameless; upright; just; godliness)

DEUTERRONOMY 6:24. And the Lord commanded us to do all these statutes, to fear the Lord our God, for our good always, that he might preserve us alive, as it is this day.

25. And it shall be our righteousness, if we observe to do all these commandments before the Lord our God, as he hath commanded us.

II SAMUEL 22:21. The Lord rewarded me according to my righteousness: according to the cleanness of my hands hath he recompensed me

22. For I have kept the ways of the Lord, and have not wickedly departed from my God.

23. For all his judgments were before me: and as for his statutes, I did not depart from them.

24. I was also upright before him, and kept myself from mine iniquity.

25. Therefore the Lord hath recompensed me according to my righteousness; according to my cleanness in his eye sight.

PSALM 4:5. Offer the sacrifices of righteousness, and put your trust in the Lord.

PSALM 11:7. For the righteous Lord loveth righteousness; his countenance doth behold the upright.

PSALM 15:1. Lord, who shall abide in thy tabernacle? Who shall dwell in thy holy hill?

2. He that walketh uprightly, and worketh righteousness, and speaketh the truth in his heart.

PSALM 23:3. He restoreth my soul: he leadeth me in the paths of righteousness for his name's sake.

PSALM 45:7. Thou lovest righteousness, and hatest wickedness: therefore God, thy God, hath anointed thee with the oil of gladness above thy fellows.

PSALM 96:13. ...he shall judge the world with righteousness, and the people with his truth.

PSALM 106:3. ...Blessed are they that keep judgment, and he that doeth righteousness at all times.

PROVERBS 10:2. ...righteousness delivereth from death.

PROVERBS 11:5. The righteousness of the perfect shall direct his way:
6. The righteousness of the upright shall deliver them:

PROVERBS 21:12. He that followeth after righteousness and mercy findeth life, righteousness, and honour.

ISAIAH 26:9. ...when thy judgments are in the earth, the inhabitants of the world will learn righteousness.

ISAIAH 32:17. And the work of righteousness shall be peace; and the effect of righteousness quietness and assurance for ever.

ISAIAH 46:12. Hearken unto me, ye stouthearted that are far from righteousness:

13. I bring near my righteousness; it shall not be far off, and my salvation shall not tarry:

ISAIAH 51:7. Hearken unto me, ye that know righteousness, the people in whose heart is my law;

ISAIAH 54:14. In righteousness shalt thou be established: thou shalt be far from oppression; for thou shalt not fear: and from terror; for it shall not come near thee.

EZEKIEL 18:20. The soul that sinneth, it shall die. ...the righteousness of the righteous shall be upon him, and the wickedness of the wicked shall be upon him.

21. But if the wicked will turn from all his sins that he hath committed, and keep all my statutes, and do that which is lawful and right, he shall surely live, he shall not die.

22. All his transgressions that he hath committed, they shall not be mentioned unto him: in his righteousness that he hath done he shall live.

23. "Have I any pleasure at all that the wicked should die," saith the Lord God, "and not that he should return from his ways, and live?"

24. But when the righteous turneth away from his righteousness, and committeth iniquity, and doeth according to all the abominations that the wicked man doeth, shall he live? All his righteousness that he hath done shall not be mentioned: in his trespass that he hath trespassed, and in his sin that he hath sinned, in them shall he die.

25. Yet ye say, the way of the Lord, is not equal. Hear now, O house

of Israel; is not my way equal? Are not your ways unequal?

26. When a righteous man turneth away from his righteousness, and committeth iniquity, and dieth in them; for his iniquity that he hath done shall he die.

27. Again, when the wicked man turneth away from his wickedness that he hath committed, and doeth that which is lawful and right, he shall save his soul alive.

28. Because he considereth, and turneth away from all his transgressions that he hath committed, he shall surely live, he shall not die.

EZEKIEL 33:12. Therefore, thou son of man, say unto the children of thy people, The righteousness of the righteous shall not deliver him in the day of his transgression: as for the wickedness of the wicked, he shall not fall thereby in the day that he turneth from his wickedness; neither shall the righteous be able to live for his righteousness in the day that he sinneth.

13. When I shall say to the righteous, that he shall surely live; if he trust to his own righteousness, and commit iniquity, all his righteousness shall not be remembered; but for his iniquity that he hath committed he shall die for it.

18. When the righteous turneth from his righteousness, and committeth iniquity, he shall even die thereby.

HOSEA 10:12. Sow to yourselves in righteousness, reap in mercy; break up your fallow ground: for it is time to seek the Lord, till he come and rain righteousness upon you.

ZEPHANIAH 2:3. Seek ye the Lord, all ye meek of the earth, which have wrought his judgment; seek righteousness, seek meekness: it may be ye shall be hid in the day of the Lord's anger.

MATTHEW 5:6. Blessed are they which do hunger and thirst after righteousness: for they shall be filled.

20. For I say unto you, that except your righteousness shall exceed the righteousness of the scribes and Pharisees, ye shall in no case enter into the kingdom of heaven.

MATTHEW 6:33. But seek ye first that kingdom of God, and his righteousness; and all these things shall be added unto you.

ROMANS 3:18. There is no fear of God before their eyes.

19. Now we know that what things so ever the law saith, it saith to them who are under the law: that every mouth may be stopped, and all

the world may become guilty before God.

20. Therefore by the deeds of the law there shall no flesh be justified in his sight: for by the law is the knowledge of sin.

21. But now the righteousness of God without the law is manifested, being witnessed by the law and the prophets;

22. Even the righteousness of God which is by faith of Jesus Christ unto all and upon all them that believe: for there is no difference:

23. For all have sinned, and come short of the glory of God;

24. Being justified freely by his grace through the redemption that is in Christ Jesus:

25. Whom God hath set forth to be a propitiation through faith in his blood, to declare his righteousness for the remission of sins that are past, through the forbearance of God;

26. To declare, I say, at this time his righteousness: that he might be just, and the justifier of him which believeth in Jesus.

ROMANS 4:3. For what saith the scriptures? Abraham believed God, and it was counted unto him for righteousness.

5. But to him that worketh not, but believeth on him that justifieth the ungodly, has faith is counted for righteousness.

ROMANS 10:3. ...they being ignorant of God's righteousness, and going about to establish their own righteousness, have not submitted themselves unto the righteousness of God.

4. For Christ is the end of the law for righteousness to every one that believeth.

6. ...the righteousness which is of faith speaketh on this wise...

9. ...if thou shalt confess with thy mouth the Lord Jesus, and shalt believe in thine heart that God hath raised him from the dead, thou shalt be saved.

10. For with the heart man believeth unto righteousness; and with the mouth confession is made unto salvation.

ROMANS 14:17. For the kingdom of God is not meat and drink; but righteousness and peace, and joy in the Holy Ghost.

I JOHN 3:7. Little children, let no man deceive you: he that doeth righteousness is righteous, even as he is righteous.

10. In this the children of God are manifest, and the children of the devil: whosoever doeth not righteousness is not of God, neither he that loveth not his brother.

"HUMBLE" (meek' submissive; subservient)

PSALM 9:12. ...he forgetteth not the cry of the humble.

MICAH 6:8. He hath shewed thee, O man, what is good; and what doth the Lord require of thee, but to do justly, and to love mercy, and to walk humble with thy God?

MATTHEW 18:4. Whosoever therefore shall humble himself as this little child, the same is greatest in the kingdom of heaven.

I PETER 5:5. ...God resisteth the proud, and giveth grace to the humble.

"CONTRITE" (broken and bruised in spirit by a sense of sin; humble; penitent))

HONOR" (respectful regard according to, or deserved by high worth; high esteem; worship)

I SAMUEL 2:30. Wherefore the Lord God of Israel saith, "...them that honor me I will honor, and they that despite me shall be lightly esteemed."

PSALM 89:7. God is greatly to be feared in the assembly of the saints, and to be had in reverences of all them that are about him.

HEBREWS 12:9. Furthermore we have had fathers of our flesh which corrected us, and we gave them reverence: shall we not much rather be in subjection unto the Father of spirits, and live?

28. Wherefore we, receiving a kingdom which cannot be moved, let us have grace, whereby we may serve God acceptably with reverence and godly fear;

"JUST" (upright; faithful; equitable)

II SAMUEL 23:3. The God of Israel said...He that ruleth over men must be just, ruling in the fear of God.

JOB 9:2. ...how should man be just with God?

3. If he will contend with him, he cannot answer him one of a thousand.

4. He is wise in heart, and mighty in strength: who hath hardened himself against him, and hath prospered?

PROVERBS 4:18. But the path of the just is as the shining light, that shineth more and more unto the perfect day.

PROVERBS 9:9. …teach a just man, and he will increase in learning.

PROVERBS 10:20. The tongue of the just is as choice silver;

PROVERBS 17:26. Also to punish the just is not good, nor to strike princes for equity.

PROVERBS 20:7. The just man walketh in his integrity;

PROVERBS 21:15. It is joy to the just to do judgment…

ISAIAH 26:7. The way of the just is uprightness…

PSALM 34:18. The Lord is nigh unto them that are of a broken heart; and saveth such as be of a contrite spirit.

ISAIAH 57:15. For thus saith the high and lofty One that inhabited eternity, whose name is Holy; I dwell in the high and holy place, with him also that is of a contrite and humble spirit, to revive the spirit of the humble, and to revive the heart of the contrite ones.

ISAIAH 66:2. For all those things hath mine hand made, and all those things have been, saith the Lord: but to this man will I look even to him that is poor and of a contrite spirit, and trembleth at my word.

"IMPENITENT" (not sorry for ones sins; hardened in sin; unrepentant)

ROMANS 2:5. But after thy hardness and impenitent heart treasurest up unto thyself wrath against the day of wrath and revelation of the righteous judgment of God;

Who will render to every man according to his deeds:

"IDOL" (an image of a divinity or a God used as an object or medium of worship. A person or thing too greatly loved or adored.)

LEVITICUS 19:4. Turn ye not unto idols, nor make to yourselves molten Gods: I am the lord your God.

LEVITICUS 26:1. Ye shall make you no idols nor graven image, neither rear you up a standing image, neither shall ye set up any image of stone in your land, to bow down unto it: for I am the Lord your God.

PSALM 97:7. Confounded be all they that serve graven images that boast themselves of idols: worship him, all ye Gods.

ISAIAH 2:8. Their land also is full of idols; they worship the work of their own hands, that which their own fingers have made:

18. And the idols he shall utterly abolish.

EZEKIEL 14:6. Therefore say unto the house of Israel, Thus saith the Lord God: Repent, and turn yourselves from your idols; and turn away your face from all your abominations.

7. For every one...which separateth himself from me, and setteth up his idols in his heart, and putteth the stumbling block of his iniquity before his face, and cometh to a prophet to inquire of him concerning me; I the Lord will answer him by myself:

EZEKIEL 18:5. But if a man be just, and do that which is lawful and right,

6. And hath not eaten upon the mountains, neither hath lifted up his eyes to the idols of the house of Israel, neither hath defiled his neighbor's wife, neither hath come near to a menstruous woman,

7. And hath not oppressed any, but hath restored to the debtor his pledge, hath spoiled none by violence, hath given his bread to the hungry, and hath covered the naked with a garment;

8. He that hath not given forth upon usury, neither hath taken any increase, that hath withdrawn his hand from iniquity, hath executed true judgment between man and man,

9. Hath walked in my statues, and hath kept my judgments, to deal truly; he is just, he shall surely live, saith the Lord God.

HABAKKUK 2:4. ...but the just shall live by faith.

LUKE 15:7. ...I say unto you, that likewise joy shall be in heaven over one sinner that repenteth, more than over ninety and nine just persons, which need no repentance.

"BLASPHEMY: BLASPHEME: BLASPHEMER" (profanity, impiety, or irreverence in speaking of God or sacred things) (deny the being or providence of God; to talk irreverently or sacrilegiously)

MATTHEW 12:31. Wherefore I say unto you, all manner of sin and blasphemy shall be forgiven unto men: but the blasphemy against the Holy Ghost shall not be forgiven unto men.

MARK 3:28. Verily I say unto you, all sins shall be forgiven unto the sons of men, and blasphemies wherewith so ever they shall blaspheme:

29. But he that shall blaspheme against the Holy Spirit hath never forgiveness, but is in danger of eternal damnation:

30. Because they said, He hath an unclean spirit.

"UNGODLY" wicked; sinful; unholy; having no likeness to God))

PSALM 1:4. The ungodly are not so; but are like the chaff which the wind driveth away.

5. Therefore the ungodly shall not stand in the judgment, nor sinners in the congregation of the righteous.

6. For the Lord knoweth the way of the righteous: but the way of the ungodly shall perish.

PROVERBS 16:27. An ungodly man diggeth up evil: and in his lips there is as a burning fire.

I PETER 4:18. And if the righteous scarcely be saved, where shall the ungodly and the sinner appear?

19. Wherefore let them that suffer according to the will of God commit the keeping of their souls to him in well-doing, as unto a faithful Creator.

II PETER 2:6. And turning the cities of Sodom and Gomorrah into ashes condemned them with an overthrow, making them an ensample unto those that after should live ungodly;

II PETER 3:7. But the heavens and the earth, which are now, by the same word, are kept in store, reserved unto fire against the Day of Judgment and perdition of ungodly men.

JUDE 4. For there are certain men crept in unawares, who were before of old ordained to this condemnation, ungodly men, turning the grace of our God into lasciviousness, and denying the only Lord God, and our Lord Jesus Christ.

14. ...Behold, the Lord cometh with ten thousands of his saints,

15. To execute judgment upon all, and to convince all that are ungodly among them of all their ungodly deeds which they have ungodly committed, and of all their hard speeches which ungodly sinners have spoken against him.

16. These are murmurers, complainers, walking after their own lusts; and their mouth speaketh great swelling words, having men's persons in admiration because of advantage.

18. How that they told you there should be mockers in the last time,

who should walk after their own ungodly lusts.

19. These be they who separate themselves, sensual, having not the Spirit.

I TIMOTHY 1:9. Knowing this, that the law is not made for a righteous man, but for the lawless and disobedient, for the ungodly and for sinners, for unholy and profane, for murderers of fathers and murderers of mothers, for manslayers,

10. For whoremongers, for them that defile themselves with mankind, for menstealers, for liars, for perjured persons, and if there be any other thing that is contrary to sound doctrine;

11. According to the glorious gospel of the blessed God...

"UNBELIEF" (lack of positive faith or belief; skepticism)

ROMANS 3:3. For what if some did not believe? Shall their unbelief make the faith of God without effect?

4. God forbid: yea, let God be true, but every man a liar; as it is written, that thou mightest be justified in thy sayings, and mightest overcome when thou art judged.

ROMANS 11:19. Thou wilt say then, the branches were broken off, that I might be grafted in.

20. Well; because of unbelief they were broken off, and thou standest by faith. Be not high-minded, but fear:

21. For if God spared not the natural branches, take heed lest he also spare not thee.

22. Behold therefore the goodness and severity of God: on them which fell, severity; but toward thee, goodness, if thou continue in his goodness: otherwise thou also shalt be cut off.

23. And they also, if they abide not still in unbelief, shall be grafted in: for God is able to graft them in again.

29. For the gifts and calling of God are without repentance.

30. For as ye in times past have not believed God, yet have now obtained mercy through their unbelief:

31. Even so have these also now not believed, that through your mercy they also may obtain mercy.

32. For God hath concluded them all in unbelief, that he might have mercy upon all.

I TIMOTHY 1:13. Who was before a blasphemer, and a persecutor, and injurious: but I obtained mercy, because I did it ignorantly in unbelief.

HEBREWS 3:12. Take heed, brethren, lest there be in any of you an evil heart of unbelief, in departing from the living God.

18. And to who swear he that they should not enter into his rest, but to them that believed not?

19. So we see that they could not enter in because of unbelief.

HEBREWS 4:9. There remaineth therefore a rest to the people of God.

10. For he that is entered into his rest, he also hath ceased from his own works, as God did from his.

11. Let us labour therefore to enter into that rest, lest any man fall after the same example of unbelief.

12. For the word of God is quick, and powerful, and sharper than any two-edged sword, piercing even to dividing asunder of soul and spirit, and of the joints and marrow, and is discerner of the thoughts and intents of the heart.

"BACKSLIDING" (gradually turning away from a religion once believed in; turning to sin)

JEREMIAH 2:19. Thine own wickedness shall correct thee, and thy backslidings shall reprove thee;

JEREMIAH 3:14. Turn, O backsliding children, saith the Lord; for I am married unto you;

JEREMIAH 14:7. ...our backslidings are many; we have sinned against thee.

"LUST" (sinful and impure desire)

PSALM 81:12. So I gave them up unto their own hearts' lust: and they walked in their own counsels.

MARK 4:18. And these are they which are sown among thorns; such as hear the word,

19. And the cares of this world, and the deceitfulness of riches, and the lusts of other things entering in, choke the word, and it becometh unfruitful.

ROMANS 1:27. And likewise also the men, leaving the natural use of the woman, burned in their lust one toward another;

ROMANS 7:7. ...for I had not known lust, except the law had said,

Thou shalt not covet,

GALATIANS 5:24. ...And they that are Christ's have crucified the flesh with the affections and lusts.

I TIMOTHY 6:9. But they that will be rich fall into temptation and a snare, and into many foolish and hurtful lusts, which drown men in destruction and perdition.

"MALICE" (evil intention to injure others; deliberate mischief; spite)

I CORINTHIANS 5:8. Therefore let us keep the feast, not with old leaven, neither with the leaven of malice and wickedness; but with the unleavened bread of sincerity and truth.

I CORINTHIANS 14:20. Brethren, be not children in understanding: howbeit in malice be ye children, but in understanding be men.

EPHESIANS 4:31. Let all bitterness, and wrath, and anger, and clamour, and evil speaking, be put away from you, with all malice:

32. And be ye kind one to another, tenderhearted, forgiving one another, even as God for Christ's sake hath forgiven you.

TITUS 3:3. For we ourselves also were sometimes foolish, disobedient, deceived, serving diver's lusts and pleasures, living in malice and envy, hateful, and hating one another.

4. But after that the kindness and love of God our Saviour toward man appeared,

5. Not by works of righteousness which we have done, but according to his mercy he saved us, by the washing of regeneration, and renewing of the Holy Ghost;

I PETER 2:1. Wherefore laying aside all malice, and all guile, and hypocrisies, and envies, and all evil speaking,

2. ...desire the sincere milk of the word that ye may grow thereby:

"MOCK" (to ridicule)

II CHRONICLES 26:16. ...they mocked the messengers of God, and despised his words, and misused his prophets, until the wrath of the Lord arose against his people, till there was no remedy.

PROVERBS 1:24. Because I have called, and ye refused; I have stretched out my hand, and no man regarded;

25. But ye have set at naught all my counsel, and would none of my reproof:

26. I also will laugh at your calamity; I will mock when your fear cometh;

PROVERBS 14:9. Fools make a mock at sin:

JUDE 17. But, beloved, remember ye the words which were spoken before of the apostles of our Lord Jesus Christ;

18. How that they told you there should be mockers in the last time, who should walk after their own ungodly lusts.

19. These be they who separate themselves, sensual, having not the Spirit.

"OFFEND" (to displease or make angry; vex or annoy)

MATTHEW 18:6. But who so shall offend one of these little ones which believe in me, it were better for him that millstones were hanged about his neck, and that he were drowned in the depth of the sea.

7. Woe unto the world because of offences! for it must needs be that offences come; but woe to that man by whom the offence cometh!

JAMES 2:10. For whosoever shall keep the whole law, and yet offend in one point, he is guilty of all.

"OPPRESS" (to burden; crush by hardships or severity; to overpower; suppress; make dispirited)

EXDOUS 23:9. ...thou shalt not oppress a stranger;

PROVERBS 14:31. He that opresseth the poor reproacheth his Maker;

ISAIAH 49:26. And I will feed them that oppress thee with their own flesh...and all flesh shall know that I the Lord am thy Saviour and thy Redeemer, the mighty One of Jacob.

MICAH 2:1. Woe to them that devise iniquity, and work evil upon their beds! When the morning is light, they practice it, because it is in the power of their hand.

2. And they covet fields, and take them by violence; and houses, and take them away: so they oppress a man and his house, even a man and his heritage.

ZECHARIAH 7:9. Thus speaketh the Lord of hosts, saying, Execute true judgment, and show mercy and compassion every man to his brother:

10. And oppress not the widow, nor the fatherless, the stranger, nor the poor; and let none of you imagine evil against his brother in your heart.

MALACHI 3:5. And I will come near to you to judgment; and I will be a swift witness against the sorcerers, and against the adulterers, and against false swearers, and against those that oppress the hireling in his wages, the widow, and the fatherless, and that turn aside the stranger from his right, and fear not me, saith the Lord of hosts.

ACTS 10:38. How God anointed Jesus of Nazareth with the Holy Ghost and with power: who went about doing good, and healing all that were oppressed of the devil; for God was with him.

"PERSECUTE" (to pursue in order to injure or afflict; harass or ill-treat)

MATTHEW 5:11. Blessed are ye, when men shall revile you, and persecute you, and shall say all manner of evil against you falsely, for my sake.

12. Rejoice, and be exceeding glad: for great is your reward in heaven: for so persecuted they the prophets which were before you.

43. Ye have heard that it hath been said; Thou shalt love thy neighbor, and hate thine enemy.

44. But I say unto you, Love your enemies, bless them that curse you, do good to them that hate you, and pray for them which despitefully use you, and persecute you;

45. That ye may be the children of your Father which is in heaven....

"REBEL" (to revolt against any authority)

JOSHUA 1:18. Whosoever he be that doth rebel against thy commandment, and will not hearken unto thy words in all that thou commandest him, he shall be put to death;

I SAMUEL 12:14. If ye will fear the Lord, and serve him, and obey his voice, and not rebel against the commandment of the Lord, then shall both ye and also the king that reigneth over you continue following the Lord your God.

15. But if ye will not obey the voice of the Lord, but rebel against the commandment of the Lord, then shall the hand of the Lord be against you, as it was against your fathers.

JOB 24:13. They are of those that rebel against the light; they know not the ways thereof, nor abide in the paths thereof.

PSALM 5:10. Destroy thou them, O God; let them fall by their own counsels; cast them out in the multitude of their transgressions; for they have rebelled against thee.

ISAIAH 1:2. ...I have nourished and brought up children, and they have rebelled against me.

20. But if ye refuse and rebel, ye shall be devoured with the sword: for the mouth of the Lord hath spoken it.

ISAIAH 63:10. But they rebelled, and vexed his holy spirit: therefore he was turned to be their enemy, and he fought against them.

"CARNAL" (pertaining to the body and its appetites; sensual; fleshly)

ROMANS 8:6. For to be carnally minded is death; but to be spiritually minded is life and peace.

7. Because the carnal mind is enmity against God: for it is not subject to the law of God, neither indeed can be.

8. So then they that are in the flesh cannot please God.

"CHARITY" (universal love and .good will)

I CORINTHIANS 13:1. Though I speak with the tongues of men and of angels, and have not charity, I am become as sounding brass, or a tinkling cymbal.

2. And though I have the gifts of prophecy, and understand all mysteries, and all knowledge; and though I have all faith, so that I could remove mountains, and have not charity, I am nothing.

3. And though I bestow all my goods to feed the poor, and though I gave my body to be burned, and have not charity, it profiteth me nothing.

4. Charity suffereth long, and is kind; charity envieth not; charity vaunteth not itself, is not puffed up.

5. Doth not behave itself unseemly, seeketh not her own, is not easily provoked, thinketh no evil;

6. Rejoiceth not in iniquity, but rejoiceth in the truth;

7. Beareth all things, believeth all things, hopeth all things, endureth all things.

8. Charity never faileth: but whether there be prophecies, they shall fail; whether there be tongues, they shall cease; whether there be knowledge, it shall vanish away.

9. For we know in part, and we prophesy in part.

13. And now abideth faith, hope, charity, these three; but the greatest of these is charity.

I CORINTHIANS 14:1. Follow after charity, and desire spiritual gifts…

COLOSSIANS 3:14. And above all these things put on charity, which is the bond of perfectness.

<u>"IN RIGHTEOUSNESS" (rectitude; rightness of intention and action; honest)</u>

LEVITICUS 19:15. Ye shall do no unrighteousness in judgment: thou shalt not respect the person of the poor, nor honour the person of the mighty: but in righteousness shalt thou judge thy neighbour.

ISAIAH 5:16. But the Lord of hosts shall be exalted in judgment, and God that is holy shall be sanctified in righteousness.

ISAIAH 42:6. I the lord have called thee in righteousness and will hold thine hand, and will keep thee, and give thee for a covenant of the people, for a light of the Gentiles;

ISAIAH 45:13. I have raised him up in righteousness, and I will direct all his ways: he shall build my city, and he shall let go my captives, not for price nor reward saith the Lord of hosts.

22. Look unto me, and be ye saved, all the ends of the earth: for I am God, and there is none else.

23. I have sworn by myself, the word is gone out of my mouth in righteousness, and shall not return, that unto me every knee shall bow, every tongue shall swear.

24. Surely, shall one say, in the Lord have I righteousness and strength: even to him shall men come; and all that are incensed against him shall be ashamed.

JEREMIAH 4:2. And thou shalt swear, the Lord liveth, in truth, in judgment, and in righteousness; and the nations shall bless themselves in him, and in him shall they glory.

HOSEA 2:19. And I will betroth thee unto me for ever; yea, I will betroth thee unto me in righteousness, and in judgment, and in loving kindness, and in mercies.

HOSEA 10:12. Sow to yourselves in righteousness, reap in mercy; break up your fallow ground: for it is time to seek the Lord, till he come and rain righteousness upon you.

ZECHARIAH 8:8. And I will bring them and they shall dwell in the midst of Jerusalem: and they shall be my people, and I will be their God, in truth and in righteousness.

EPHESIANS 4:22. That ye put off concerning the former conversation the old man, which is corrupt according to the deceitful lusts;

23. And be renewed in the spirit of your mind;

24. And that ye put on the new man, which after God is created in righteousness and true holiness.

REVELATIONS 19:11. And I saw heaven opened, and behold a white horse; and he that sat upon him was called Faithful and true, and in righteousness he doth judge and make war.

"A WOMAN'S HAIR IS HER GLORY"

I CORINTHIANS 11:5. But every woman that prayeth or prophesieth with her head uncovered dishonoureth her head;

6. For if the woman be not covered let her also be shorn:

15. But if women have long hair, it is a glory to her: for her hair is given her for a covering.

"THY SHALT NOT EAT SWINE NOR TOUCH ITS' DEAD CARCASE"

DEUTERONOMY 14:8. And the swine, because it divideth the hoof, yet cheweth not the cud, it is unclean unto you: ye shall not eat of their flesh, nor touch their dead carcass.

"FELLOWSHIPPING WITH UNBELIEVERS"

II CORINTHIANS 6:14. Be ye not unequally yoked together with unbelievers: for what fellowship hath righteousness with unrighteousness? And what communion hath light with darkness?

15. And what concord hath Christ with Belial? Or what part hath he that believeth with an infidel?

16. And what agreement hath the temple of God with idols? For ye are the temple of the living God; as God hath said, I will dwell in them, and walk in them; and I will be their God, and they shall be my people.

17. Wherefore come out from among them, and be ye separate, saith the Lord, and touch not the unclean thing; and I will receive you,

18. And will be a Father unto you, and ye shall be my sons and daughters...

"WORSHIPPING ANOTHER GOD"

I CORINTHIANS 10:20. But I say that the things which the Gentiles sacrifice, they sacrifice to devils, and not to God: and I would not that ye should have fellowship with devils.

21. Ye cannot drink the cup of the Lord, and the cup of devils: ye cannot be partakers of the Lord's Table, and of the table of devils.

"DO NOT SHUT YOUR HEART TO THE CRY OF THE HUNGRY"

PSALM 41:1. Blessed is he that considereth the poor: the Lord will deliver him in time of trouble.

ISAIAH 58:6. Is not this the fast that I have chosen?...

7. Is it not to deal thy bread to the hungry, and that thou bring the poor that are cast out to thy house? When thou seest the naked, that thou cover him;

EZEKIEL 18:5. But if a man be just, and do that which is lawful and right,

7. ...hath given his bread to the hungry, and hath covered the naked with a garment;

9. ...he shall surely live, saith the Lord God.

"GREIVING FOR THE DEAD"

MATTHEW 22:29. Jesus answered and said unto them, ye do err, not knowing the scriptures, nor the power of God.

30. For in the resurrection they neither marry, nor are given in marriage, but are as angels of God in heaven.

"NO FEAR OF GOD"

EXODUS 20:20. ...for God is come to prove you, and that his fear may be before your faces, that ye sin not.

DEUTERONOMY 4:10. Specially the day that thou stoodest before the Lord thy God in Horeb, when the Lord said unto me, Gather me the people together, and I will make them hear my words, that they may learn to fear me all the days that they shall live upon the earth, and that they may teach their children.

DEUTERONOMY 5:29. O that there were such an heart in them, that they would fear me, and keep all my commandments always, that it might be well with them, and with their children for ever.

DEUTERONOMY 6:13. Thou shalt fear the Lord thy God, and serve him, and shall swear by his name.

II KINGS 17:39. But the Lord your God ye shall fear; and he shall deliver you out of the hand of all your enemies.

PSALM 25:12. What man is he that feareth the Lord? Him shall he teach in the way that he shall choose.

PSALM 34:9. O fear the Lord, ye his saints: for there is no want to them that fear him.

PSALM 85:9. Surely his salvation is nigh them that fear him...

PSALM 111:5. He hath given meat unto them that fear him...
10. The fear of the Lord is the beginning of wisdom.

PROVERB 1:7. The fear of the Lord is the beginning of knowledge...

PROVERB 3:7. Be not wise in thine own eyes: fear the Lord, and depart from evil.

PROVERBS 10:27. The fear of the Lord prolongeth days...

PROVERBS 15:16. Better is little with the fear of the Lord than great treasure and trouble therewith.

PROVERBS 19:23. The fear of the Lord tendeth to life: and he that hath it shall abide satisfied; he shall not be visited with evil.

PROVERBS 31:30. ...a woman that feareth the Lord, she shall be praised.

ECCLESIASTES 3:14. I know that, whatsoever God doeth, it shall be for ever: nothing can be put to it, nor any thing taken from it: and God doeth it, that men should fear before him.

ECCLESIASTES 8:12. Though a sinner do evil an hundred times and his days be prolonged, yet surely I know that it shall be well with them that fear God, which fear before him:

ECCLESIASTES 12:13. Let us hear the conclusion of the whole matter: Fear God, and keep his commandments: for this is the whole duty of man.

II CORENTHIANS 7:1. Having therefore these promises, dearly beloved, let us cleanse ourselves from all filthiness of the flesh and spirit, perfecting holiness in the fear of God.

MALACHI 4:2. But unto you that fear my name shall the Sun of righteousness arise with healing in his wings; and ye shall go forth, and grow up as calves of the stall.

"NO PRAISE FOR GOD"

DEUTERONOMY 10:21. He is thy praise and he is thy God,

PSALM 22:23. Ye that fear the Lord, praise him...
26. ...they shall praise the Lord that seek him...

PSALM 33:1. Rejoice in the Lord O ye righteous: for praise is comely for the upright.

PSALM 50:23. Whoso offereth praise glorified me...

PSALM 66:2. Sing forth the honour of his name: make his praise glorious.

PSALM 100:4. Enter into his gates with thanksgiving, and into his courts with praise: be thankful unto him, and bless his name.

5. For the Lord is good; his mercy is everlasting; and his truth endureth to all generations.

PSALM 113.3. From the rising of the sun unto the going down of the same the Lord's name is to be praised.

"HATRED FOR ANOTHER PERSON"

MATTHEW 7:1. Judge not, that ye be not judged.

2. For with what judgment ye judge, ye shall be judged: and with what measure ye mete, it shall be measured to you again.

3. Why beholdest thou the mote that is in thy brother's eye, but considerest not the beam that is in thine own eye?

4. Or how wilt thou say to thy brother, Let me pull out the mote out of thine eye; and, behold, a beam is in thine own eye?

5. Thou hypocrite, first cast out the beam out of thine own eye; and then shalt thou see clearly to cast out the mote out of thy brother's eye.

JOHN 7:24. Judge not according to the appearance, but judge righteous judgment.

"WALKING IN THE FLESH"

MATTHEW 5:27. Ye have heard that it was said by them of old time, Thou shalt not commit adultery:

28. But I say unto you, that whosoever looketh on a woman to lust after her hath committed adultery with her already in his heart.

29. And if thy right eye offends thee, pluck it out, and cast it from thee: for it is profitable for thee that one of thy members should perish, and not that thy whole body should be cast into hell.

30. And if thy right hand offend thee, cut it off, and cast it from thee: for it is profitable for thee that one of thy members should perish, and not that thy whole body should be cast into hell.

ROMANS 8:1. There is therefore now no condemnation to them which are in Christ Jesus, who walk not after the flesh, but after the Spirit.

4. That the righteousness of the law might be fulfilled in us...

5. For they that are after the flesh do mind the things of the flesh; but they that are after the Spirit the things of the Spirit.

6. For to be carnally minded is death; but to be spiritually minded is life and peace.

12. Therefore, brethren, we are debtors, not to the flesh, to live after the flesh.

13. For if ye live after the flesh, ye shall die: but if ye through the Spirit do mortify the deeds of the body, ye shall live.

ROMANS 13:13. Let us walk honestly, as in the day; not in rioting and drunkenness, not in chambering and wantonness, not in strife and envying.

14. But put ye on the Lord Jesus Christ, and make not provision for the flesh, to fulfill the lusts thereof.

I CORINTHIANS 1:26. For ye see your calling, brethren, how that not many wise men after the flesh, not many mighty, not many noble, are called:

29. That no flesh should glory in his presence.

GALATIANS 5:13. For, brethren, ye have been called unto liberty; only use not liberty for an occasion to the flesh, but by love serve one another.

16. This I say then, Walk in the Spirit, and ye shall not fulfill the lust of the flesh.

17. For the flesh lusteth against the Spirit, and the Spirit against the

flesh: and these are contrary the one to the other: so that ye cannot do the things that ye would.

19. Now the works of the flesh are manifest, which are these: Adultery, fornication, uncleanness, lasciviousness.

20. Idolatry, witchcraft, hatred, variance, emulations, wrath, strife, seditions, heresies.

21. Envyings, murders, drunkenness, revellings, and such like...they which do such things shall not inherit the kingdom of God.

24. And they that are Christ's have crucified the flesh with the affections and lusts.

25. If we live in the Spirit, let us also walk in the Spirit.

II PETER 2:9. The Lord knoweth how to deliver the godly out of temptations, and to reserve the unjust unto the day of judgment to be punished.

10. But chiefly them that walk after the flesh in the lust of uncleanness, and despise government. Presumptuous are they, self-willed, they are not afraid to speak evil of dignities.

12. But these, as natural brute beasts, made to be taken and destroyed, speak evil of the things that they understand not; and shall utterly perish in their own corruption;

13. And shall receive the reward of unrighteousness, as they that count it pleasure to riot in the day time. Spots they are and blemishes, sporting themselves with their own deceivings while they feast with you;

14. Having eyes full of adultery and that cannot cease from sin; beguiling unstable souls: an heart they have exercised with covetous practices; cursed children:

15. Which have forsaken the right way, and are gone astray, following the way of Balaam the son of Bosor, who loved the wages of unrighteousness;

17. These are wells without water, clouds that are carried with a tempest; to whom the mist of darkness is reserved for ever.

20. ...if after they have escaped the pollutions of the world through the knowledge of the Lord and Saviour Jesus Christ, they are again entangled therein, and overcome, the latter end is worse with them than the beginning.

21. For it had been better for them not to have known the way of righteousness, than, after they have known it, to turn from the holy commandment delivered unto them.

22. But it is happened unto them according to the true proverb, the dog is turned to his own vomit again; and the sow that was washed to her wallowing in the mire.

"PROUD IN HEART AND SPIRIT"

PSALM 12:3. The Lord shall cut off all flattering lips, and the tongue that speaketh proud things:

PSALM 101:5. ...him that hath a high look and a proud heart will not I suffer.

PSALM 119:21. Thou hast rebuked the proud that are cursed, which do err from thy commandments.

PROVERBS 15:25. The Lord will destroy the house of the proud...

PROVERBS 16:5. Every one that is proud in heart is an abomination to the Lord: though hand joins in hand, he shall not be unpunished.

18. Pride goeth before destruction and a haughty spirit before a fall.

PROVERBS 28:25. He that is of a proud heart stirreth up strife...

ECCLESIASTES 7:8. ...the patient in spirit is better than proud in spirit.

ISAIAH 2:12. For the day of the Lord of hosts shall be upon every one that is proud and lofty, and upon every one that is lifted up; and he shall be brought low:

ISAIAH 13:11. ...I will cause the arrogance of the proud to cease, and will lay low the haughtiness of the terrible.

MALACHI 4:1. For, behold, the day cometh, that shall burn as an oven; and all the proud, yes, and all that do wickedly, shall be stubble: and the day that cometh shall burn them up, saith the Lord of hosts, that it shall leave them neither root nor branch.

"GOSSIPING ABOUT OTHERS" (TALEBEARING)

PSALM 101:5. Whoso privily slandereth his neighbor, him will I cut off.

I CORINTHIANS 15:33. Be not deceived: evil communications corrupt good manners.

"UNFORGIVENESS - KNOWN OR UNKNOWN"

MATTHEW 6:14. For if ye forgive men their trespasses, your heavenly Father will also forgive you:

15. But if ye forgive not men their trespasses, neither will your Father forgive your trespasses.

LUKE 17:3. Take heed to yourselves: If thy brother trespass against thee, rebuke him; and if he repent, forgive him.

4. And if he trespass against thee seven times in a day, and seven times in a day turn again to thee, saying, I repent; thou shalt forgive him.

MATTHEW 18:21. Then came Peter to him, and said, Lord, how often shall my brother sin against me, and I forgive him? Till seven times?

22. Jesus saith unto him, I say not unto thee, until seven times; but, until seventy times seven.

II CORINTHIANS 2:10. To whom ye forgive any thing, I forgive also: for if I forgave any thing, to whom I forgave it, for your sakes forgave I it in the person of Christ;

11. Lest Satan should get an advantage of us...

"ANGER - KNOWN OR UNKNOWN"

PSALM 37:8. Cease from anger, and forsake wrath:

PROVERBS 14:17. He that is soon angry dealeth foolishly...

PROVERBS 29:22. An angry man stireth up strife and a furious man aboundeth in transgression.

ECCLESIASTES 7:9. Be not hasty in thy spirit to be angry: for anger resteth in the bosom of fools.

MATTHEW 5:22. But I say unto you, that whosoever is angry with his brother without a cause shall be in danger of the judgment...

"LYING" (speaking falsely about anyone or anything)

PSALM 31:18. Let the lying lips be put to silence; which speak grievous things proudly and contemptuously against the righteous.

PROVERBS 6:16. These...things the Lord hates:

17. ...a lying tongue...

REVELATION 21:8. ...all liars, shall have their part in the lake which burneth with fire and brimstone...

REVELATION 22:15. For without are...whosoever loveth and maketh a lie.

"UNJUST TREATMENT TOWARDS OTHERS"

PROVERBS 11:7. ...the hope of unjust men perisheth.

PROVERBS 28:8. He that be usury and unjust gain increaseth his substance; he shall gather it for him that will pity the poor.

II PETER 2:9. The Lord knoweth how to deliver the Godly out of temptations, and to reserve the unjust unto the day of judgment to be punished...

"SLOTHFULNESS"

PROVERBS 18:9. He also that is slothful in his work is brother to him that is a great waster.

PROVERBS 19:15. Slothfulness casteth into a deep sleep; and an idle soul shall suffer hunger.

24. A slothful man hideth his hand in his bosom, and will not so much as bring it to his mouth again.

PROVERBS 21:25. The desire of the slothful killeth him; for his hands refuse to labour.

"FOOLISH THINKING, ACTING, OR SPEAKING"

PROVERBS 12:23... ...the heart of fools proclaimeth foolishness.

PROVERBS 14:24. ...the foolishness of fools is folly.

PROVERBS 19:3. The foolishness of man perverteth his way: and his heart fretteth against the Lord.

PROVERBS 24:9. The thought of foolishness is sin...

ECCLESIASTES 10:12. ...the lips of a fool will swallow up himself.

13. The beginning of the words of his mouth is foolishness: and the end of his talk is mischievous madness.

"COVET" (selfish desire for another's possession)

EXODUS 20:17. Thou shalt not covet thy neighbour's house; thou shalt not covet thy neighbour's wife, nor his manservant, nor his maidservant, nor his ox, nor his ass, nor any thing that is thy neighbour's.

ACTS 20:33. I have coveted no man's silver, or gold, or apparel.

"COVETOUSNESS" (desirous; .grasping; avaricious - eager to possess and to keep riches; greedy for gain)

PSALM 119:36. Incline my heart unto thy testimonies, and not to covetousness.

PROVERBS 28:16. ...he that hateth covetousness shall prolong his days...

JEREMIAH 22:17. But thine eyes and thine heart are not but for thy covetousness...

HABAKKUK 2:9. Woe to him that coveteth an evil covetousness to his house, that he may set his nest of high, that he may be delivered from the power of evil:...

MARK 7:22. Thefts, covetousness, wickedness, deceit, lasciviousness, an evil eye, blasphemy, pride, foolishness:

23. All these evil things come from within, and defile the man.

LUKE 12:15. And he said unto them, take heed, and beware of covetousness: for a man's life consisteth not in the abundance of the things which he possesseth.

EPHESIANS 5:3. But fornication, and all uncleanness, or covetousness, let it not be once named among you, as becometh saints;

COLOSSIANS 3:5. Mortify therefore your members which are upon the earth; fornication, uncleanness, inordinate affection, evil concupiscence, and covetousness, which is idolatry:

6. For which things' sake the wrath of God cometh on the children of disobedience:

HEBREWS 13:5. Let your conversation be without covetousness; and be content with such things as ye have: for he hath said, I will never leave thee, nor forsake thee.

II PETER 2:3. And through covetousness shall they with feigned words make merchandise of you:

"CRUEL" (inhuman; unfeeling; without kindly qualities)

Proverbs 11:17. ...HE THAT IS CRUELTROUBLETH HIS OWN FLESH.

"ENVY" (discontent or resentment because of another's success, advantage or superiority)

JOB 5:2. ...envy slayeth the silly one.

PROVERBS 14:30. Let not thine heart envy sinners...

PSALM 37:1. Fret not thyself because of evildoers, neither be thou envious against the workers of iniquity.

PROVERBS 24:1. Be not thou envious against evil men, neither desire to be with them.

"DOUBT" (hesitates to believe; distrust; question)

MATTHEW 21:21. Jesus answered and said unto them, Verily I say unto you, if ye have faith, and doubt not, ye shall not only do this which is done to the fig tree, but also if ye shall say unto this mountain, be thou removed, and be thou cast into the sea; it shall be done.

"FALSE WITNESS"

EXODUS 20:16. Thou shalt not bear false witness against thy neighbour.

DEUTERONOMY 19:16. If a false witness rises up against any man to testify against him that which is wrong;

17. Then both the men, between whom the controversy is, shall stand before the Lord, before the priests and the judges, which shall be in those days;

18. And the judges shall make diligent inquisition: and, behold, if the witness be a false witness, and hath testified falsely against his brother;

19. Then shall ye do unto him, as he had thought to have done unto his brother: so shalt thou put the evil away from among you.

PROVERBS 6:16. These...things doth the Lord hate...

19. A false witness that speaketh lies.

PROVERBS 19:5. A false witness shall not be unpunished...

PROVERBS 21:28. A false witness shall perish:

MATTHEW 15:19. For out of the heart proceed evil thoughts, murders, adulteries, fornications, thefts, false witness, and blasphemies:
20. These are the things which defile a man...

"HYPOCRISY" (a pretending to be what one is not)

ISAIAH 32:6. For the vile person will speak villainy, and his heart will work iniquity, to practice hypocrisy, and to utter error against the Lord, to make empty the soul of the hungry, and he will cause the drink of the thirsty to fail.

MATTHEW 23:28. Even so ye also outwardly appear righteous unto men, but within ye are full of hypocrisy and iniquity.

LUKE 21:1. In the mean time, when there were gathered together an innumerable multitude of people, insomuch that they trod one upon another, he began to say unto his disciples, first of all, Beware ye of the leaven of the Pharisees, which is hypocrisy.

I TIMOTHY 4:1. Now the Spirit speaketh expressly, that in the latter times some shall depart from the faith, giving heed to seducing spirits, and doctrines of devils;
2. Speaking lies in hypocrisy...

I PETER 2:1. Wherefore laying aside all malice, and all guide, and hypocrisies, and envies, and all evil speaking.
2. As newborn babes, desire the sincere milk of the word that ye may grow thereby:

"HYPOCRITE" (one who practices deception to gain his own end)

JOB 8:13. ...and the hypocrite's hope shall perish...

JOB 15:34. For the congregation of hypocrites shall be desolate...

JOB 20:4. Knowest thou not this of old, since man was placed upon earth,
5. That the triumphing of the wicked is short, and the joy of the hypocrite but for a moment?

JOB 27:8. For what is the hope of the hypocrite, though he hath gained, when God taketh away his soul?

PROVERBS 11:9. A hypocrite with his mouth destroyeth his neighbor...

ISAIAH 9:17. Therefore the Lord shall have no joy in their young men; neither shall have mercy on their fatherless and widows: for every one is a hypocrite and an evildoer...

ISAIAH 33:14. ...fearfulness hath surprised the hypocrites.

MATTHEW 23:13. But woe unto you, scribes and Pharisees, hypocrites! For ye shut up the kingdom of heaven against men: for ye neither go in yourselves, neither suffer ye them that are entering to go in.

14. Woe unto you, scribes and Pharisees, hypocrites! For ye devour widows' houses, and for a pretence make long prayer: therefore ye shall receive the greater damnation.

15. Woe unto you, scribes and Pharisees, hypocrites! For ye compass sea and land to make one proselyte, and when he is made, ye make him twofold more the child of hell than yourselves.

23. Woe unto you, scribes and Pharisees, hypocrites! For ye pay tithe of mint and anise and cumin, and have omitted the weightier matters of the law, judgment, mercy, and faith: these ought ye to have done, and not to leave the other undone.

25. Woe unto you, scribes and Pharisees, hypocrites! For ye make clean the outside of the cup and of the platter, but within they are full of extortion and excess.

27. Woe unto you, scribes and Pharisees, hypocrites! For ye are like unto whited sepulchers, which indeed appear beautiful outward, but are within full of dead men's bones, and of all uncleanness.

28. Even so ye also outwardly appear righteous unto men, but within ye are full of hypocrisy and iniquity.

29. Woe unto you, scribes and Pharisees, hypocrites! Because ye build the tombs of the prophets, and garnish the sepulchers of the righteous.

30. And say, if we had been in the days of our fathers, we would not have been partakers with them in the blood of the prophets.

33. Ye serpents, ye generation of vipers, how can ye escape the damnation of hell?

"MURMUR" (to mutter in discontent; grumble)

EXODUS 16:8. And Moses said...for that the Lord heareth your murmurings which ye murmur against him: and what are we? Your murmurings are not against us, but against the Lord.

NUMBERS 11:1. And when the people complained, it displeased the Lord: and the Lord heard it; and his anger was kindled; and the fire of the Lord burnt among them, and consumed them that were in the uttermost parts of the camp.

2. And the people cried unto Moses; and when Moses prayed unto the Lord, the fire was quenched.

4. And the mixed multitude that was among them fell a-lusting: and the children of Israel also wept again. And said who shall give us flesh to eat?

5. We remember the fish, which we did eat in Egypt freely; the cucumbers, and the melons, and the leeks, and the onions, and the garlic:

6. But now our soul is dried away: there is nothing at all, beside this manna, before our eyes.

16. And the Lord said unto Moses…

18. …say thou unto the people, Sanctify yourselves against tomorrow, and ye shall eat flesh: for ye have wept in the ears of the Lord, saying, who shall give us flesh to eat? For it was well with us in Egypt: therefore the Lord will give you flesh and ye shall eat.

20. …even a whole month, until it comes out at your nostrils, and it be loathsome unto you: because that ye have despised the Lord which is among you, and have wept before him, saying, Why came we forth out of Egypt?

33. And while the flesh was yet between their teeth, ere it was chewed, the wrath of the Lord was kindled against the people, and the Lord smote the people with a very great plague.

NUMBERS 12:1. And Miriam and Aaron spoke against Moses because of the Ethiopian woman whom he had married…

4. And the Lord spoke suddenly unto Moses, and unto Aaron, and unto Miriam, Come out ye three unto the tabernacle of the congregation.

6. And he said hear now my words: If there be a prophet among you, I the Lord will make myself known unto him in a vision, and will speak unto him in a dream.

7. My servant Moses is not so, who is faithful in all mine house.

8. With him will I speak mouth to mouth, even apparently, and not in dark speeches; and the similitude of the Lord shall he behold: wherefore then were ye not afraid to speak against my servant Moses?

9. And the anger of the Lord was kindled against them; and he departed.

10. …and, behold, Miriam became leprous, white as snow…

11. And Aaron said unto Moses, Alas, my Lord, I beseech thee; lay not the sin upon us, wherein we have done foolishly, and wherein we have sinned.

13. And Moses cried unto the Lord, saying, Heal her now, O God, I beseech thee.

14. And the Lord said unto Moses, if her father had but spit in her face, should she not be ashamed seven days? Let her be shut out from the camp seven days, and after that let her be received in again.

I CORINTHIANS 10:1. Moreover, brethren, I would not that ye should be ignorant, how that all our fathers were under the cloud, and all passed through the sea.

2. And were all baptized unto Moses in the cloud and in the sea;

3. And did all-eat the same spiritual meat;

4. And did all drink the same spiritual drink: for they drank of the spiritual Rock that followed them: and that Rock was Christ.

5. But with many of them God was not pleased: for they were overthrown in the wilderness.

6. Now these things were our examples, to the intent we should not lust after evil things, as they also lusted.

7. Neither be ye idolaters, as were some of them; as it is written, the people sat down to eat and drink, and rose up to play.

8. Neither let us commit fornication, as some of them committed, and fell in one day three and twenty thousand.

9. Neither let us tempt Christ, as some of them also tempted, and were destroyed of serpents.

10. Neither murmur ye, as some of them also murmured, and were destroyed of the destroyer.

11. Now all these things happened unto them for ensamples: and they are written for our admonition, upon whom the ends of the world are come.

12. Wherefore let him that thinketh he standeth take heed lest he fall.

BOOK V

JUST *"QUOTES"*

This book contains "words to live by" that were spoken to her by her Father over a period of several years, and others He had her to record as she heard them to help her to grow in the Spirit as He wanted her to. It is her desire that they will also be of value to you and help you in your spiritual growth.

"God cannot inhabit an unclean vessel"

"Doubt means that your mind doesn't understand"

"Unbelief denies God: Brings disgrace upon him"

"God sometimes deliver us out of temptation, from temptation, through temptation"

"The devil offers you glory without suffering, but ends up giving you suffering without glory"

Two reasons why you will miss heaven:

Blasphemy - those who have said that the works of God are of Satan. And those who have said that the works of Satan are of God.

Those who have waited one day too late

"Hope is a substance of faith"

"Unbelief sees God through circumstances"

"Religion can blind your mind to the simple things of the word of God"

"God will always require obedience. He will get his way"

"Don't doubt in the dark what God has given you in the light"

"The fear of God is to hate evil"

"Our purpose here is to glorify God and to build character"

"The function of the law was never to provide salvation, but to make us aware of our need for it"

"Is the law against God's promises? No!!"

"How do we know that we are truly born of God?

***I JOHN 5:1.** Whosoever believeth that Jesus is the Christ is born of God:*

18. We know that whosoever is born of God sinneth not; but he that is begotten of God keepeth himself, and that wicked one toucheth him not.

20. And we know that the Son of God is come, and hath given us an understanding, that we may know him that is true, and we are in him that is true, even in his Son Jesus Christ. This is the true God, and eternal life."

"True sonship with God"

I JOHN 3:4. *Whosoever committeth sin transgressed also the law: for sin is the transgresses of the law.*

5. And ye know that he was manifested to take away our sins; in him is no sin.

6. Whosoever abideth in him sinneth not: whosoever sinneth hath not seen him, neither known him.

7. ...he that doeth righteousness is righteous, even as he is righteous.

8. He that committeth sin is of the devil; for the devil sinneth from the beginning.

9. Whosoever is born of God doth not commit sin; for his seed remaineth in him: and he cannot sin, because he is born of God.

10. In this the children of God are manifest, and the children of the devil: whosoever doeth not righteousness is not of God, neither he that loveth not his brother.

"Paul was content with weakness. It allowed him to step back and let God take over."

Essentials for fellowship with Christ-

Obedience (will)

Love (heart)

Truth (mind)

Why don't we enjoy the Lord?

We do not know him

We have a wrong view of God's attitude toward us

We cannot accept our acceptance by him

We live with guilt (which may be false)

"Get Jesus at the center of your life, and he will take care of the circumference."

Three reasons why some people are not healed -

Their stubborn will

Their bitterness and unforgiveness against others (attitudes)

We choose to violate the divine guidance for out health.

"God would never let you suffer if it did not accomplish a purpose in your life."

"Faith without righteous living is dead"

"The best protection one can have against the onslaught of the devil is a humble heart"

"If you are saved, this earth is the only hell that you will ever have. If

you are lost, this earth is the only heaven you will ever know"

"The Lord's compassion never fails"

"The Lord's faithfulness never diminishes, It is always great. Tied to his immutability"

"Do not compromise the word of God"

"You may bruise the devil's head, but he will bust yours"

"If you make a petition with any other God, you will go to the lion's den"

"We must not seek the gift. We must seek the giver"

"See yourself from God's viewpoint, and you will stop worrying"

"To worry is to be pagan"

"If we continue to do wrong, we set in motion a string of consequences"

"The Lord's mercies never cease"

"When you are born again, you take on the nature of God"

"In company guard your tongue. In solitude, your thoughts"

"Many who pray for a change in circumstances, really ought to pray for a change in character"

"God allows temptation in order to temper us, never to trip us"

"God Cannot do any more for you than he can do through you"

"God will not change your will against your will"

"I give up that which I cannot keep to gain that which I cannot lose"

"The trouble with life is that it is daily. What are you doing with your life? Commit is to God"

"The fear of God takes care of every other fear"

"A tree is best measured when it is down" (one's character)

'The presence of God dispels darkness"

"When one is conquered and ruled by God, they are saved"

"What life does to us depends upon what life finds in us"

"Trails do not discover the source of our joys, difficulties, circumstances, character, they reveal them"

"The kingdom of God is the reign of God in our hearts"

"What we are suppose to do with time here on earth can never be done in eternity" (redeem the time)

"Old sins have long shadows"

"You love Jesus Christ as much as you love the least of these" (other people)

"When God develops a character, he is never in a hurry"

"If God was still working in the churches the way he used to, there would be a lot of work for the undertaker"

"The real way to God is giving up your thinking"

"Christ in me is my forgiving power. Christ in me is my releasing power"

"Delay is not God's denial for our prayers"

"It is strong faith that gives glory to God"

"Walk comes before talk"

"Reason with the facts"

"God's love is not conditioned upon a response. He loves all, even those who are going to hell. Biblical love is unconditional"

"I do not live by explanations, I live by promises"

"The more you use your faith, the stronger it will become"

"How to get rid of unbelief / doubt - simply choose to believe God"

"The traitor is within us, not without. The enemy is us"

"The gospel - Jesus came, died, and rose again, Understanding the gospel mixed with faith, brings about new life"

"The law of God is the mind of God. It came from the heart of God. God is greater than the law and is able to enable us to perform it. (walk in the righteousness of the law). No one will be able to live righteous by the law alone."

"Put on the Lord Jesus Christ, and do not walk in the flesh"

"One of God's characteristics is reliability"

"To be filled with God is to be empty of self"

"You cannot believe beyond actual knowledge"

"Your body belongs to God. You have no right to defile it"

"Give all that you have to God, and trust him to give to you all that you need"

"The church is the only place where the soldiers are killing each other"

"If you were translated to heaven today, you would be no closer to God than you are now"

"The Lord in heaven loves you too much to harm you, and he is too wise to make a mistake"

"Heaven is a prepared place for a prepared people"

"When you learn how to trust boundaries, God will give you horizons"

"Doubt is a protection for that which you already believe"

"If a Christian does not heed to the conviction of the Holy Spirit, he is disciplined, chastised. Rejection to chastisement leads to death. There comes a time when God gets tired of fooling with us" (sons of prediction?)

"Two things that displease Jesus -

Hypocrisy

Unbelief- believing something that is contrary to God's word. Anything that is contrary to what God has spoken, is from Satan"

"Jesus only killed two things on earth -

Hogs

Fig tree"

"Repent or perish"

"The word of God is our only rule of conduct, our final authority, and cannot be discerned by the natural mind"

"Wisdom is seeing things from God's point of view"

"We are the sons of God in the Son of God"

"If you knew everything, what would you think about?"

"The will of God is expensive. If we do not obey it, we pay dearly"

"God has already supplied every need that you could ever have need of. All you have to do is to trust and obey, and he will supply them as you need them"

"When you pray, remember that God is not in the bargaining business. All of the promises that he has made to us were established before the foundation of the world and are immutable" (unchangeable)

"Suffering is not only meant to burn out the dross, but to burn in the promises"

"The Holy Spirit which comes into your heart teaches you how to talk to the Father" (pray)

"Jesus gave me his faith, and by it I received salvation"

"Let us be as watchful after the victory, as we were during the battle"

"Just remember, when the devil reminds you of your past, remind him of his future"

"Be patient with each other when mistakes are made. God is not through with us yet"

"The way to sin is paved with an anticipation of failure"

"Salvation by being good or works? No!! It is simply by trusting in Jesus" (believe on the Lord Jesus Christ, and you shall be saved)

"Satan will do everything he can to keep you off of your knees, even if it's only adjusting a window shade"

"A faith that cannot be tested, cannot be trusted"

"The world cannot breed a lion that God cannot tame"

"God will never abandon his purpose for our lives—to make us like Christ"

"Grow in grace so that you will not grow in disgrace"

"You are not what you think you are, but you are what you think"

"When you work for the devil, you get wages. The wages of sin is death. When you work for God you get a gift, eternal life"

"God forgives us our sins and remembers them no more. Or casts them in a sea of forgetfulness. But he does not cancel out the harvest of sorrows. Neither does this negate the law of, "Whatsoever you sow, so shall you also reap""

"You can buy back anything that the devil has taken from you, if you are willing to pay the price"

"Only pigs like pig pen, straying sons do not. They will come home"

"God is in control over every situation"

"We have inclined our ears to listen to the devil and not to God"

"Whatever you focus your attention on; you will be dominated by it"

"Anything that comes between our soul and God becomes our idol"

"Try Jesus, if you do not like him, Satan is always happy to take you back"

"You cannot forgive that which you cannot forget"

"Words are like chickens, they always come home to roost"

"Prayer is not trying to get God to do something for us. It is bringing our will under the submission of God's will"

"There is always a payday"

"God never answers the ways or the when's"

"If we do not trust Jesus as our Lord and saviour, we will spend eternity in hell"

"You will have whatsoever you sayeth!"

"Look to the cross and live"

"When the request is not right, God says, no

When the time is not right, God says, slow.

When you are not right, God says, grow.

When everything is right, God says, go"

"Do not keep your eyes upon the storm, keep them upon Jesus"

"It is wrong speaking that releases the ability of the devil"

"God will allow anything to come into your life that you will allow"

"Accept the will of God and it will make you. Reject the will of God and it will break you"

"Make a decision to walk in the love of God"

"Forgiving is Jesus' work. God wants to set you free so that you can bless others"

"You are required to give your humanness to god so he can work through you"

"Learn to trust in the indwelling Spirit of Christ to do that which seems impossible"

"When a man forgets himself, he usually does something that others will remember"

"Satan cannot do anything to you that you will not allow him to do"

"God would never trust you with troubles, if he did not have grace sufficient enough to bring you out of them"

"God will not do anything that you should not do"

"When you are doing something for the Lord you do not have to worry about the obstacles. Just keep on serving the Lord and see how things work out for you. You have the option of worrying or trusting"

"It is the tender heart that produces the trusting heart"

"The tender heart became the heart that believed God for many things"

"ALL OF LIFE IS DEALING WITH GOD, NOT WITH PEOPLE"

"It is in dying, not doing, that produces spiritual fruit"

"God may permit the devil to delay his plans, but he cannot change them"

"Let the Holly Spirit pray through you for the things that he wants to bring into your life, so that he can give them to you"

"Learn to depend on the indwelling Christ of God. Depend upon the word of God in the ordinaries of life"

"Anger is the hot wind that blows out the cool wind of reasoning"

'The law of vision -

What we see, that we shall think

What we think, that we shall conceive

What we conceive, that we shall bring forth"

"Faith is an act of the will"

"I have nothing to prove. I have someone to please"

ACTS 17:26. AND HATH MADE OF ONE BLOOD ALL NATIONS OF MEN FORTO DWELL ON ALLTHE FACE OF THE EARTH...v 27. THAT THEY SHOULD SEEK THE LORD. IF HAPLY THYE MIGHT FEEL AFTER HIM. AND FIND HIM, THOUGH HE BE NOT FAR FROM EVERY ONE OF US: v. 28 FOR IN HEM WE LIVE, AND MOVE, AND HAVE OUR BEING...FOR WE ARE ALSO HIS OFFSPRING.
EVERY THING THAT WE DO TO OURSELVES OR TO OTHERS WE DO IT UNTO GOD. EVERY ACT WE COMMIT IN MIND, BODY, OR SPIRIT, BE IT GOOD OR BAD, WE CAUSE GOD TO PARTICIPATE IN IT. WOE!! ALL SCRIPTURE REFERENCES ARE FROM THE KING JAMES VERSION OF THE BIBLE.

THE GATES OF HELL *OPENED?*

Scientists are afraid that they have opened the gates to hell. A geological group who drilled a hole about 14.4 kilometers deep (about 9 miles) in the crust of the earth, are saying that they heard human screams. Screams have been heard from the condemned souls from earth's deepest hole. Terrified scientists are afraid they have let loose the evil powers of hell up to the earth's surface.

"The information we gathering is so surprising, that we are sincerely afraid of what we might find down there," stated Mr. Azzacov, the manager of the project to drill a 14.4 kilometer hole in remote Siberia.

The geologists were dumbfounded. After they had drilled several kilometers through the earth's crust, the drill bit suddenly began to rotate wildly. "There is only one explanation – that the deep center of the earth is hollow," the surprised Azzacov explained. The second surprise was the high temperature they discovered in the earth's center. "The calculations indicate the given temperature was about 1,100 degrees Celsius, or over 2,000 degrees Fahrenheit," Dr. Azzacov points out. "This is far more than we expected. It seems almost like an Inferno of fire is brutally going on in the center of the earth."

"The last discovery was nevertheless the most shocking to our ears, so much so that the scientists are afraid to continue the project. We tried to listen to the earth's movements at certain intervals with supersensitive microphones, which were let down through the hole. What we heard turned those logically thinking scientists into a trembling ruins. It was sometimes a weak, but high pitched sound which we thought to be coming from our own equipment," explained Dr. Azzacov. "But after some adjustments we comprehended that indeed the sound came from the earth's interior. We could hardly believe our own ears. We heard a human voice, screaming in pain. Even though one voice was discernible, we could hear thousands, perhaps millions, in the background, of suffering souls screaming. After this ghastly discovery, about half of the scientists quit because of fear. Hopefully, that which is down there will stay there," Dr. Azzacov added.

Translated from AMMENUSASTIA, a newspaper published in Finland.

NUMBERS 11:14, 16 & 17

TEACH THE CHILDREN

THE MOST EXPENSIVE THING IN THE WORLD IS SIN. ACCOUNTABILITY TO GOD IS INEVITABLE AND INESCAPABLE. I CORINTHIANS 6:18. FLEE FORNICATION (UNLAWFUL SEXUAL INTERCOURSE) TO AVOID FORNICATION. LET EVERY MAN HAVE HIS OWN WIFE, AND EVERY WOMAN HER OWN HUSBAND. (I CORINTHIANS 7:2) DEEDS OF THE FLESH REAP A BITTER HARVEST.

HAVE YOU CONSIDERED THE FINALITY OF DEATH? THERE WILL NOT BE A SECOND CHANCE AFTER YOU HAVE LEFT THIS PRESENT LIFE. ALL OF LIFE IS DEALING WITH GOD NOT WITH PEOPLE. THE PROPER FEAR OF GOD WILL KEEP YOU FROM SIN. GOD CANNOT INHABIT AN UNCLEAN VESSEL.

MATH 6:24 NO MAN CAN SERVE TWO MASTERS.

THERE ARE TWO REASONS WHY YOU WILL MISS HEAVEN: BLASPHEMY AND THOSE WHO HAVE WAITED ONE DAY TOO LATE. REPENT ALL YE LAND!! PREPARE YE THE WAY FOR THE LORD!!

HATE IS TOO GREAT A BURDEN TO BEAR!

IT DESTROYS ONLY THE ONE WHO CARRIES IT WITHIN.

DECEMBER 1996, 3:30 AM – TELL THEM, I AM COMING SOON!!

READ - A DEVINE REVELATION OF HELL by Mary Baxter. REVELATION 21:8. BUT THE FEARFUL, AND UNBELIEVING, AND THE ABOMINABLE, AND MURDERERS, AND WHOREMONGERS, AND SOCERERS, AND IDOLATERS, AND ALL LIARS, SHALL HAVE THEIR PART IN THE LAKE WHICH BURNETH WITH FIRE AND BRIMESTONE: WHICH IS THE SECOND DEATH. HELL HAS NO EXITS!! YOUR BODY BELONGS TO GOD. YOU HAVE NO RIGHT TO DEFILE IT. YOU CAN GET RID OF A DESIRE, BUT YOU CANNOT UNDO AN ACT. CALL OUT TO GOD AND ASK HIM TO DO IT FOR YOU. HE WILL NOT FAIL YOU. DEEDS OF THE FLESH REAP A BITTER HARVEST.

ROMANS 12:5. SO WE, BEING MANY, ARE ONE BODY IN CHRIST, AND EVERY ONE MEMBER ONE OF ANOTHER.

ROMANS 2:17. ...THOU ARE CALLED A JEW...vs. 18 thru 28. FOR HE IS NOT A JEW, WHICH IS ONE OUTWARDLY...v 29. BUT HE IS A JEW, WHICH IS ONE INWARDLY...KJV.

CPSIA information can be obtained
at www.ICGtesting.com
Printed in the USA
LVOW02s0806100617
537661LV00009B/40/P

9 781480 905511